Using Microsoft Explorer
on the Internet

BOOKS AVAILABLE

Using Microsoft Explorer on the Internet

by

P.R.M. Oliver
and
N. Kantaris

BERNARD BABANI (publishing) LTD
THE GRAMPIANS
SHEPHERDS BUSH ROAD
LONDON W6 7NF
ENGLAND

PLEASE NOTE

Although every care has been taken with the production of this book to ensure that any projects, designs, modifications and/or programs, etc., contained herewith, operate in a correct and safe manner and also that any components specified are normally available in Great Britain, the Publishers and Author(s) do not accept responsibility in any way for the failure (including fault in design) of any project, design, modification or program to work correctly or to cause damage to any equipment that it may be connected to or used in conjunction with, or in respect of any other damage or injury that may be so caused, nor do the Publishers accept responsibility in any way for the failure to obtain specified components.

Notice is also given that if equipment that is still under warranty is modified in any way or used or connected with home-built equipment then that warranty may be void.

© 1997 BERNARD BABANI (publishing) LTD

First Published - January 1997

British Library Cataloguing in Publication Data:

A catalogue record for this book is available from the
British Library

ISBN 0 85934 419 3

Cover Design by Gregor Arthur
Cover illustration by Adam Willis
Printed and Bound in Great Britain by Cox & Wyman Ltd, Reading

ABOUT THIS BOOK

Using Microsoft Explorer on the Internet has been written to help you get to grips with the Internet and e-mail in general and with browsing, or surfing, the World Wide Web with Microsoft's Internet Explorer in particular.

These days you can't read a paper, listen to the radio, or watch television very long before you hear or see mention of the Internet, or the Information Superhighway. It has become an integral part of our lives over the last couple of years. What importance will it have after the next few years? If it follows the current trend and carries on growing exponentially, it could well become the most important technical development in the history of mankind. So as not to get completely left behind we feel that everyone should test the water, but beware, the Web can be very habit forming.

An attempt has been made not to use too much 'jargon', but with this subject, some is inevitable, so a fairly detailed glossary of terms is included, which should be used with the text where necessary.

The book starts by overviewing the short history of the Internet (from the US military to rampant commercialism) and describes how the World Wide Web fits into the general scene.

A chapter follows on the different browsers supplied by Microsoft and how you can download and install them on your PC. How to go about connecting to the Internet and obtaining the technical help that may be needed is also very briefly covered. The book was written using version 3.0 of the Internet Explorer, working under Windows 95.

The following chapters describe the current version 3.0 of Internet Explorer and how best to use it for surfing the Web and for handling your e-mail and your Newsgroup activities.

Chapters are included on how to find your way around the Web using some of the many search 'engines' that are available, and how to recognise and guard against some of the unfortunate behaviour traits that have developed with the Internet.

One thing to remember when reading the book is that the whole Internet scenario is changing every day, especially the World Wide Web. What is there to look at today, may have gone, or changed shape, by tomorrow.

The book does not describe how to set up your PC, or how to use Microsoft Windows. If you need to know more about the Windows environment, then we suggest you select an appropriate level book from the 'Books Available' list - these books are loosely graduated in complexity from the less demanding *one step at a time* series, to the more detailed *explained* series. They are all published by BERNARD BABANI (publishing) Ltd.

Like the rest of our computer series, this book was written with the busy person in mind. It is not necessary to learn all there is to know about a subject, when reading a few selected pages can usually do the same thing quite adequately. With the help of this book, it is hoped that you will be able to come to terms with the Internet, Microsoft Explorer and the World Wide Web and get the most out of your computer in terms of efficiency, productivity and enjoyment, and that you will be able to do it in the shortest, most effective and informative way.

ABOUT THE AUTHORS

Phil Oliver graduated in Mining Engineering at Camborne School of Mines in 1967 and since then has specialised in most aspects of surface mining technology, with a particular emphasis on computer related techniques. He has worked in Guyana, Canada, several Middle Eastern countries, South Africa and the United Kingdom, on such diverse projects as: the planning and management of bauxite, iron, gold and coal mines; rock excavation contracting in the UK; international mining equipment sales and international mine consulting for a major mining house in South Africa. In 1988 he took up a lecturing position at Camborne School of Mines (part of Exeter University) in Surface Mining and Management.

Noel Kantaris graduated in Electrical Engineering at Bristol University and after spending three years in the Electronics Industry in London, took up a Tutorship in Physics at the University of Queensland. Research interests in Ionospheric Physics, led to the degrees of M.E. in Electronics and Ph.D. in Physics. On return to the UK, he took up a Post-Doctoral Research Fellowship in Radio Physics at the University of Leicester, and then in 1973 a lecturing position in Engineering at the Camborne School of Mines, Cornwall, (part of Exeter University), where since 1978 he has also assumed the responsibility for the Computing Department.

ACKNOWLEDGEMENTS

We would like to thank colleagues at the Camborne School of Mines for the helpful tips and suggestions which assisted us in the writing of this book, especially Andrew Torry who spent many patient hours (and some impatient ones too!) getting Windows 95 and the Microsoft Internet Explorer to recognise our Local Area Network. Without this help we would not have been able to continue.

We would also like to thank Microsoft for making this excellent software available free of charge, or commitment, on the Internet.

TRADEMARKS

CONTENTS

1. THE INTERNET

What is the Internet? - A Brief History

In the mid 1960s with the cold war very prominent in the Northern Hemisphere, the US military faced a strange strategic problem. How could the country successfully communicate after a possible nuclear war? They would need a command and control communication network linking the cities, states and military bases, etc. But, no matter how the network was protected it would always be vulnerable to the impact of a nuclear attack and if the network had a control centre it would be the first to go.

As a solution, the concept was developed that the network itself should be assumed to be unreliable at all times and should be designed to overcome this unreliability. To achieve this, all the nodes of the network would be equal in status, each with its own authority to originate, pass, and receive messages. The messages themselves would be divided into small parts, or packets, with each being separately addressed. The transmission of each packet of data would begin at a specified source node, and end at another specified destination node, but would find its own way through the network, with the route taken being unimportant. With this concept, if sections of the network were destroyed, that wouldn't matter as the packets would use the surviving nodes.

The National Physical Laboratory, here in the UK, set up the first test network on these principles in 1968. Shortly afterwards, the Pentagon's Advanced Research Projects Agency (ARPA) funded a larger, more ambitious project in the USA, with the high-speed 'supercomputers' of the day as the network nodes.

In 1969, the first such node was installed in UCLA. By December of that year, there were four nodes on the infant network, which was named ARPANET, after its sponsor. The four computers could transfer data on dedicated high-speed transmission lines, and could be programmed remotely from the other nodes. For the first time, scientists and researchers could share one another's computer facilities from a long distance. By 1972 there were thirty-seven nodes in ARPANET.

It soon became apparent, however, that much of the traffic on ARPANET was not long-distance computing, but consisted of news and personal messages. Researchers were using ARPANET not only to collaborate on projects and trade ideas on work, but to socialise. They had their own personal accounts on the ARPANET computers, and their own personal addresses for electronic mail and they were very enthusiastic about this particular new service, which we shall hear much more of in later sections.

Throughout the '70s, the ARPA network grew. Its decentralised structure made expansion easy as it could accommodate different types of computers, as long as they could speak the standard packet-switching language. ARPA's original standard for communication was known as NCP short for 'Network Control Protocol', but this was soon superseded by the higher-level standard known as TCP/IP, which has survived until today.

TCP, or 'Transmission Control Protocol', converts messages into streams of packets at the source, then reassembles them back into messages at the destination. IP, or 'Internet Protocol', handles the addressing.

Over the years, ARPANET itself became a smaller and smaller part of the growing proliferation of other networked machines, but TCP/IP linked them all. As the '70s and '80s advanced, many different groups found themselves in possession of powerful computers. It was fairly easy to link these computers to the growing global network. As the use of TCP/IP, which was in the public-domain by that time, became more common, entire other networks were incorporated into the **Internet**.

In 1984 the National Science Foundation became involved and created the new NSFNET linking newer and faster supercomputers with bigger and faster links. Other US government agencies joined the bandwagon, including NASA, the National Institutes of Health and the Department of Energy.

ARPANET itself formally died in 1989, but its functions not only continued but were steadily improved. In Europe, major international 'backbone' networks started to provide connectivity to many millions of computers on a large number of other networks. Commercial network providers in both the US, Europe and Asia were beginning to offer Internet access and support on a competitive basis to any interested parties.

The extended use of the Internet cost the original founders little or nothing extra, since each new node was independent, and had to handle its own technical requirements and funding.

Today there are hundreds of thousands of nodes in the Internet, scattered throughout the world, with more coming on-line all the time and many millions of people using this often named 'Information Super Highway' every day.

Built to be indestructible and with no centralised control, it's no wonder the word 'anarchic' is often bandied around when the Internet is discussed!

Why Use the Internet?

Now we know what the Internet is, what can we use it for? Four things, basically spring to mind:

- sending and receiving e-mail messages
- taking part in discussion groups
- accessing data stored on distant computers
- transferring data and program files from and to these distant computers.

E-mail:

Electronic mail has to be the main use of the Internet. It is very much faster that letter mail, which is known as 'snailmail' by regular e-mail users. It consists of electronic text, that is transmitted, sometimes in seconds, to anywhere else in the World that is connected to a main network. E-mail can also be used to send software and other types of files which are 'attached' to your message. As we shall see in a later chapter, Internet Explorer software makes this a very easy process.

Newsgroups:

Discussion groups, or 'newsgroups,' are another feature of the Internet that are easily accessed with a good browser like the Microsoft Explorer. On the Internet they are generally known as USENET and consist of over 20,000 separate groups which let you freely participate in discussion on a vast amount of subjects. In fact almost any subject you could think of is covered, and the number of groups is growing larger all the time. Unfortunately in some of the groups many of the users seem to consist of adolescent teenagers with very little in the way of common sense or sophistication. You will see what we mean when you try exploring some of the fringe, or *alt*, for alternate groups.

Long Distance Computing:

As we saw, this was the original inspiration for ARPANET and for some, is still a very important part of the Internet. Using a program like Telnet you can maintain accounts on distant computers, run programs from them as if they were on your own PC, and generally make use of powerful supercomputers a continent away. Most major libraries now offer electronic card catalogues for free search, and CD-ROM archives of specialist data are increasingly available through this type of service.

Most games software is currently available on CD-ROM discs that you run in your own computer, but it is getting common now for game suppliers to also store information that you can access from the Internet.

File Transfers:

There is a fantastic amount of free software available over the Internet, as well as a multitude of text and graphic files of almost any subject you care to mention.

File transfers carried out with a protocol known as FTP, allow Internet users to access remote machines and retrieve these for their own use. Many Internet computers allow anyone to access them anonymously, and to simply copy their public files, free of charge. With the right connections, entire books can be transferred in a matter of minutes. With the wrong connections though, the process can take hours! Of course, many more millions of files are available to people with accounts, who are prepared to pay for them.

The Internet is in fact spawning a new form of publishing, in which the reader simply electronically copies the work on demand. Several Internet programs, such as 'Archie', 'Gopher' and 'WAIS, have been developed to explore these enormous archives of material, but using the World Wide Web these all become transparent to the end user.

The World Wide Web

Up until recently all of these activities required very expensive computing facilities and a large measure of computer literacy. Times have changed, however, and it is now possible to fairly easily and cheaply install a modem in your PC, connect to the Internet and with a World Wide Web browser, like Microsoft Explorer, carry them out with very little technical knowledge. Hence the reason for this book, to help you on your way.

The World Wide Web, WWW, W3, or Web as we shall call it, was initially developed in Switzerland by CERN (the European Laboratory for Particle Physics), to form a distributed hypermedia system. It now consists of Web client computers (yours and mine) and server computers handling multimedia documents with hypertext links built into them. Client computers use browser software (such as Microsoft Explorer) to view pages of these documents, one at a time. Server computers use Web server software to maintain the documents for us to access.

If you have used the Help pages of Microsoft Windows you are familiar with a hypertext document. It contains links that you click with the mouse pointer to jump to other information. The advantage of hypertext in a Web document is that if you want more information about a particular subject, you just click on it and another page is opened for you to read or look at. In fact, documents can be linked to other documents (or graphics) by completely different authors and stored in completely different computers; much like footnoting, but you can get the referenced document instantly!

So, to access the Web, you run a browser program, in our case Microsoft Explorer, which reads files and documents, and fetches them from other sources on the Internet into the memory of your PC.

Currently the Web offers the following through a hypertext, and in some cases, hypermedia interface:

- HTML-formatted hypertext and hypermedia documents

- Anything served through Gopher

- Anything served through WAIS (Wide-Area Information Servers)

- Anything served through anonymous FTP sites

- Full Archie services (an FTP search service)

- Full Veronica services (a Gopher search service)

- Anything on Usenet

- Anything accessible through Telnet

- Anything in hytelnet (hypertext Telnet)

- Anything in hyper-g (a networked hypertext system in use throughout Europe)

- Anything in the form of man pages (online documentation, or manual, that commonly comes bundled with computers running the UNIX operating system).

Thus Web browsers, such as Microsoft Explorer, provide users of computer networks with a consistent means to access a variety of media in a very simplified fashion.

They have changed the way people view and create information, and have formed the first true global hypermedia network. No wonder their use has taken off so dramatically in the last two years.

Hypermedia is a superset of hypertext - it is any medium with pointers to other media. This means that the latest browsers display formatted text, images, play sound clips, or even video type animations. Some of these, however, may require extra hardware, like a sound card, on your computer.

HTML - The Web Language:

You may never get involved with this, but Web documents are created by authors using a language called HTML (HyperText Markup Language). This offers short codes, or tags, to designate graphical elements and hypertext links. Clicking a link on a Web page in your browser, brings documents located on a distant server to your screen, irrespective of the server's geographic location. Documents may contain text, images, sounds, movies, or a combination of these, in other words - multimedia.

How Links are Named:

Every link in a hypertext Web document has to have a unique name and for you to use your browser properly you will need to understand about Uniform Resource Locators, or URLs. It is possible to represent nearly any file or service on the Internet with a URL and several example are given below.

The first part of the URL (before the two slashes) specifies the method of access. The second is typically the address of the computer on which the data, or service, is located. Further parts may specify the names of files, the port to connect to, or the text to search for in a database. A URL is always a single unbroken line with no spaces.

Here are some examples of URLs:

http://www.ex.ac.uk/location/book.html

This would connect to an HTTP server (a Web server) and would retrieve an HTML file (a Web file).

ftp://www.xerox.com/pub/file.txt

This would open an FTP connection to www.xerox.com and retrieve a text file.

gopher://www.hcc.hawaii.edu

This would connect to the Gopher at the distant www.hcc.hawaii.edu (A university in Hawaii).

8

file://www.ex.ac.uk/location/pic.gif

This would retrieve a picture file and display it.

file://www.ex.ac.uk/location/

This would display the directory contents of a distant location.

news:alt.sex

This would read the latest Usenet news by connecting to a specified news host and would return the articles in the alt.sex newsgroup in hypermedia format.

The first part of the URL (before the two slashes) gives the method of access at that address:

- **http** - a hypertext document or directory
- **Gopher** - a gopher document or menu
- **ftp** - a file available for downloading or a directory of such files
- **news** - a newsgroup
- **Telnet** - a computer system that you can log into from across the Internet
- **WAIS** - a database or document on a WAIS (**W**ide **A**rea **I**nformation **S**earch) database
- **file** - a file located on a local drive (like your hard drive)

Sites that run World Wide Web servers are typically named with a www. at the beginning of the network address.

As we shall see, Microsoft Explorer allows you to specify a URL and thus connect to that document, or service. When selecting hypertext links in a Web page (an HTML document), you are actually sending a request to open a URL. In this way, hyperlinks can be made not only to other texts and media, but also to other network services. Web browsers are not simply Web clients, but are also full FTP, Gopher, and Telnet clients in their own rights.

All of these features are now easily available over ordinary phone lines, once you get direct Internet access through a local Internet Provider, as explained in the next chapter.

2. INTERNET EXPLORING

At the time of writing this book, the Web browser market for Windows PCs had two main players, Netscape and Microsoft. Browsers are in fact being given away by both of these. Netscape started the trend by posting beta, or test, copies of versions of its Netscape Navigator for free download. Then it effectively made the shipping version of its browsers free downloads as well, by allowing 90 days for evaluation. To try and get into the market, Microsoft gives away all its browser products, with no mention of future payment. You will see icons similar to these on many Web pages. They are to encourage you to use that particular make of browser. If you click one of them it opens the download page for that browser type.

These companies are rushing to give away very high quality software because there's a lot of money to be made in the future. By flooding the market with their Navigator software, Netscape were able to float their company on the US stock market in record time and saw its stock price rocket to rather excessive heights. This without making a profit until after it went public and with what looked like a very unimpressive balance sheet. The fact that at the time it was the dominant player in the Internet market was enough for Wall Street.

But they both really want to dominate the Web server market. This field can stand expensive software used to create and manage Web sites on the Internet and in the booming office 'Intranet' market.

Microsoft seems to have modelled its Internet strategy on Netscape's, though somewhat later. It will be very interesting to see how the scenario unfolds over the next few years. Microsoft have made a habit up until now of dominating their markets. Look at DOS,

Windows and then the applications like Excel and Word, etc. We hope there will be enough room for both of these two major players.

Microsoft Products

At the time of writing, Microsoft have several versions of their Internet Explorer available for use, as described below. This scenario is changing very quickly, but our book is based mainly on the current version 3.0 for Windows 95

Microsoft offers Internet Explorer for the Windows 3.1, Windows 95, and Windows NT platforms, as well as for Macintosh.

Internet Explorer 2.1 for Windows 3.1:

This 16-bit very basic browser includes support for HTML tables and fonts, and for SSL 2.0 security protocol. With an add-on kit, it now includes mail, NNTP news, and all the components required to connect to the Internet, including a Sign-up wizard, a new TCP/IP stack, and a dialler.

Internet Explorer 3.0 for Windows 95:

At the time of writing this has just been released, and includes ActiveX, Java, and Netscape Plug-in support, as well as Internet conferencing and collaboration. Cascading style sheets add visual features and more control to HTML. Integrated Java Support, with fast 'Just-In-Time' compiling, provides very fast Java applet execution, and the new Scripting Support for both Microsoft's *VBScript* and Netscape's *JavaScript* languages allows communication with Java applets, ActiveX controls, and other software components such as Plug-ins.

The new 'HTTP Keep-Alive' protocol provides fast access to complex incoming Web pages by maintaining a connection until the page is fully loaded instead of establishing a separate connection for each image on the page.

With the fully integrated Mail and News features, you can create and read mail messages in formatted HTML or in plain text. Mail also supports full Web linking.

Many of the features for version 3.0 outlined above are well beyond the scope of this book.

Internet Explorer 2.0 for Macintosh:

Supports all the features of Internet Explorer 2.0 for Windows 95 as well as support for Netscape Plug-ins, and more multi-media features.

Explorer Requirements

The minimum hardware requirements to run Internet Explorer version 3.0 are the same as those for Windows 95. A 386, or higher, PC with 4 MB of RAM (but 8 MB are recommended), a VGA Display (SVGA with 256 colours or higher is recommended), and at least 6 MB of hard disc space on your C: drive. You also need a connection to the Internet, via a Modem, Ethernet Card, or ISDN direct phone line.

To run Explorer 3.0 as an on-line browser you must have a direct 32-bit Internet connection. The ability to send and receive e-mail does not necessarily mean you will be able to access the World Wide Web. There are three requirements for this:

1   A direct Ethernet connection to the net, or a dialup SLIP or PPP account from an Internet service provider.

2   A 32-bit TCP/IP stack.

3   The Microsoft Explorer software.

Getting On Line

Unless you are lucky enough to have a PC which is connected to a Local Area Network (LAN), which has Internet access, you will need a modem to be able to communicate with the rest of the world. This is a device that converts data so that it can be transmitted over the telephone system.

You will also need to find, and subscribe to, a suitable Internet provider. When we went to press, there were over 40 such providers in the UK. They can be listed on the Web by accessing the following address:

`http://thelist.iworld.com/`

and selecting the United Kingdom. Also you could try your telephone directory, or possibly adverts in a computer magazine, or in the computer section of your local paper.

What you are ideally looking for is **full dial-up SLIP or PPP connection with unlimited WWW access to the Internet**, and hopefully, this should be possible by dialling a local number to your provider's access point. (SLIP and PPP are only two communication standards that you need to have, but do not need to understand).

The local call access will mean your phone bills should not be excessive, especially if you do your Web browsing in off-peak times. The unlimited access means you will not pay any extra to your Internet Provider no matter how many hours you spend glued to Internet Explorer. Such a service will probably cost in the order of £30 to set up and about £150 per year afterwards, plus the ubiquitous VAT of course.

If you need to purchase and install a modem, your Internet Provider will probably be able to provide one, along with all the necessary cables, connections, software, help and back up that is bound to be required.

From now on in this book, we assume that you have an active connection to the Internet. Trouble shooting this is not within our remit!

Getting Your Browser

When you are actually connected to the Internet you can download Microsoft's Internet Explorer software absolutely free of charge.

If you are not yet connected, you have more of a problem getting the software. Some computer magazines that come with CD-ROMs carry some of the version 2.0 browsers, but the best thing would be to get yourself on line and connected to the Internet, as briefly described above, and using the browser supplied by your Internet provider, download what you want from Microsoft's Web pages.

A word of warning though, don't expect to be able to do this in the middle of a weekday. Microsoft's lines are normally so overcrowded that it is almost impossible to connect to them at peak times, let alone to download several MB of program files. With the recent release of their new version 3.0 browser this situation has become impossible. We downloaded our version at five o'clock on a Sunday morning, and it still took nearly an hour.

Downloading the Internet Explorer:

We will outline the procedure for downloading the Internet Explorer version 3.0 for Windows 95. This is only being distributed as a 32-bit Windows program and you must have a 32-bit TCP/IP stack to be able to use it.

Unfortunately, if you are running Windows 3.1, or 3.11, you **must** use the 'less interesting' 16-bit version of Internet Explorer 2.1 for Windows 3.1.

15

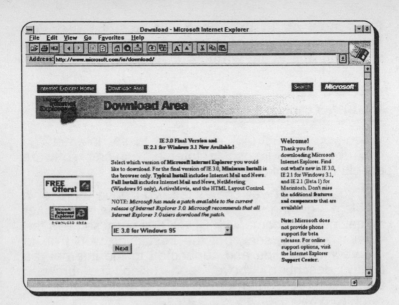

First you must access the Microsoft
Web page shown above by clicking a
Download Area button from a Web
page, or by entering the following
URL address into your browser.

http://www.microsoft.com/ie/download/

This is the page you will start from whenever you want
to download any Microsoft browser software. As things
have a habit of changing very rapidly on the Web, if the
above does not work by the time you read this, you
may have to improvise a little.

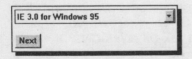

Select the program you
want to download from
the drop-down list, by
clicking the right hand
arrow and highlighting
from the list. When you have chosen, click the **Next**
button. If you are lucky, and not too many other people
are trying to do the same thing, this will open the next
page where you select the browser language you want,
which will probably be 'US English', and the version of

16

Explorer you want to download. We had the choice of three versions: **Minimal** for just the browser, **Typical** including Mail and Newsreader features, and **Full** with other more advanced features we have not covered in this book.

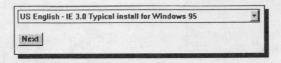

As shown above, we selected a Typical installation. When the **Next** button is clicked, you are then offered a choice of where to download from.

To speed up the transfer process you should select the fastest site, which is probably the one nearest to you. For the UK, first select Europe and then choose a suitable UK source, if there is one, or one as near as possible.

Clicking the filename entry link, and giving a file saving location when asked, will start the transfer process. It is always a good idea to have a temporary storage area on your hard disc for these occasions. Ours is a folder, or directory, called *temp*, as shown below.

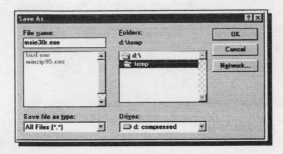

The browser file you selected should eventually arrive in your temporary folder. The procedure can be very slow. With us the 6.3MB file took over 40 minutes, or several cups of coffee.

Installing Internet Explorer:

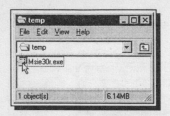

Double-clicking the down-loaded .EXE program file from a Windows 95 'My Computer' window, as shown here, will start the installation procedure.

You should first read the licence agreement and as long as you are happy with this, click the **Yes** button to start the procedure.

You are then told that you need at least 5.5MB of empty space on your C: drive. Unfortunately you do not have any choice of where the program is installed, and we had trouble completing an installation with over 20MB of free space.

Next you are asked if you want to control which parts of the Explorer suite are installed. Selecting **Yes** with the 'Typical' downloaded version gives you the following options.

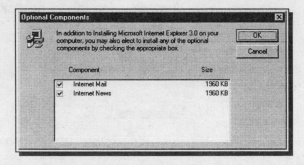

Clicking the **OK** button will start the file copy process which proceeds for several minutes while the program is installed on your system.

When this procedure is finished you will be asked to restart your computer by clicking the **Yes** button. If you did not have enough space on your hard disc, you will be told to free up more room and try again. Good luck.

Starting the Explorer

The Internet

When your system starts up again you will find a new icon, named 'The Internet', has been placed on your Desktop. Double-clicking this icon for the first time will start the Internet Connection Wizard. This will step you through the process of establishing your link to the Internet. When you have finished with a window you press **Next>** to move on, or **<Back** to return to the previous one.

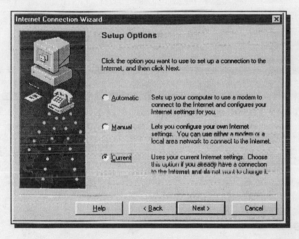

As can be seen above, if you have a modem this Wizard can make the process of setting up your connection quite painless. We were not impressed however with the facilities for connecting up via a Local Area Network. Obviously how you complete the options that are offered will depend on your particular system and circumstances.

When the Wizard has finished its work you will be asked if you want to make this your default, or main, browser. Clicking **Yes** will set the file association of Web page files so that they will always open into this particular browser.

19

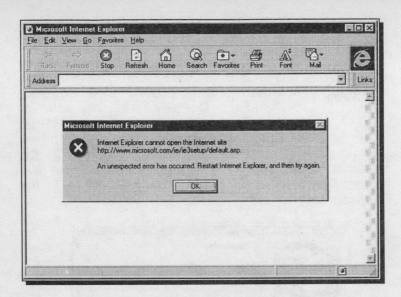

After all this procedure you then get your first look at the new browser. Hopefully not like ours, as shown above.

If you have not yet connected to the Internet, or if your connection is not satisfactory, you will get a message box similar to the one shown here, to tell you. Clicking the **OK** button will open the browser, and will load an empty file 'page', but it will obviously not be able to open any on-line Web pages until you are connected.

When the above screen dump was taken we were having trouble getting the program to accept that we had a 32-bit connection to our network. It actually took several frustrating days before we were successful!

If all is well, you should get an opening screen something like that shown on the next page.

Note that when the Explorer is actually downloading data from the network, the Stop button on the Toolbar is active, the large Status Indicator to the right of the Address text box shows with an active display, and the

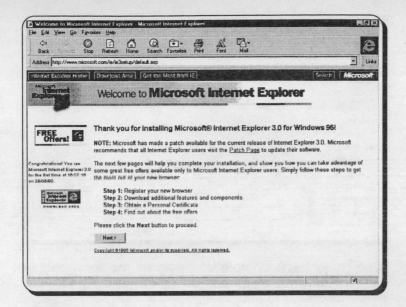

icon at the right end of the status bar gives a graphic indication of what is actually happening.

This is an opening welcome page that gives you the opportunity to download extra Explorer software, to register your copy and apply for a personal certificate.

Registering Your Software

If you are in the mood and have the time, you can step through the procedure of registering your copy of the program straight away by clicking the **Next** link button. Otherwise you can come back to this page and register later on.

The top section of the on-line registration form is shown on the next page. As long as you know your e-mail address, it is a simple matter to complete this form with your personal information. Mind you, whether you actually want to do this is a different matter. If you value your confidentiality you will probably not bother.

Register Your Copy of Microsoft Internet Explorer

By registering your copy of Microsoft Internet Explorer, you'll have the option of being notified of browser updates, be eligible to take advantage of special offers, find out about new beta software, and more! To submit your Microsoft® Internet Explorer registration, please fill in all the fields below, and then click the **Submit Registration** button at the bottom of the page.

Personal Info

E-mail address:	poliver@csm.ex.ac.uk
First name, M.I.:	Phil / R
Last name:	Oliver
Company name:	CSM
Street address:	Pool
Street address:	
City	State/Province:	Redruth / Cornwall
Postal Code	Country:	TR15 3SE / UK
Area code	Phone number:	

When you have completed filling in the form simply click the **Submit Registration** button to send all your personal details to Microsoft.

The next two Web pages opened give you access to more free goodies to download and the option to get your own Personal Certificate. If you need such a thing, fine, go ahead and get it, otherwise click the **Next** button to open the last set-up page shown below.

Cool Places To Take Your New Browser

Now that you've completed the online portion of Microsoft Internet Explorer setup, you're ready to start surfing! We've provided some useful links below to help you get started:

- **Internet Explorer Free Offers!** - Get the details on all the great free offers we've put together for Microsoft Internet Explorer users.

- **Microsoft Internet Explorer Start Page** - This is the default home page for your new browser. The Microsoft Start Page lets you create a customized home page that's just right for you. Plus, you can link to lots of exciting places all over the Web, enter contests, win prizes, and more!

- **How-To Guide** - Now that you've installed the best browser available, take it for a test drive. This step-by-step overview will let you see the features of your new browser in action, and show you how to use them.

- **Cool Sites** - A collection of Web sites that take advantage Internet Explorer features, including our weekly Top Ten Sites list.

- **Cool Controls** - Download some ActiveX controls that will bring the Web pages you visit to life.

- **Site Builder Workshop** - If you're a developer or Web author, you'll love the workshop. You can find cool ActiveX controls, HTML templates, information on tools, free software and more.

- **Internet Explorer Support Center** - A one-stop location for frequently asked questions, known issues, product feedback, in-depth technical information, and more!

- **Internet Explorer Home Page** - Be sure to add this one to your favorites! Get the latest info, support, free software, and news about Microsoft Internet Explorer.

Thank you for choosing Microsoft Internet Explorer. Happy Surfing!

Your PC Settings

Your computer probably started life set to a screen resolution of 640 X 480 pixels. It then displays a screen of 640 pixels wide and 480 pixels high on the monitor. The bigger the monitor you have, the bigger the screen resolution you can use, as everything gets smaller as the resolution goes up.

For Web browsing you want as large a resolution as you can get so that you can fit more on the screen. Web pages are almost always too large to fit on one screen. We recommend using a resolution of 800 X 600 if you have a 14" or 15" monitor, and a resolution of 1024 X 768 for 17" and larger monitors.

It is easy to change the screen settings, but time consuming, as Windows 95 must be re-started for them to take affect. Click the **Start**, button, and then **Settings**, **Control Panel**, double-click on the **Display** icon, and then click the Settings tab to open the window shown here. Both the **Color palette** and the **Desktop area** slider settings are interlinked. The higher the colour setting the lower will be the maximum Desktop area, or resolution. In our case above with a

23

High Colour (16 bit) setting our maximum resolution is 800 by 600.

With this colour setting you get near photographic image quality, and many graphics, or pictures, look much better than with only a 256 colour setting. You will find the Web much more entertaining if you surf at 64 thousand colours, instead of 256.

A Trial Run

You should now be up and running with the Internet Explorer, so let's do something. There are many millions of Web pages to look at, so where do we start? You may have started already from the last set-up page, but there is one UK institution that we all know and love, the Government! They have spent time and money on their Web presentations, so we will take a quick look.

Start Explorer, if it is not already going, and click on the Search button (on the button bar known as the Toolbar). This opens the default 'Find it Fast' search page, that at first glance can look a little daunting. Don't get worried, we will discuss this page again in a later chapter. For now type 'UK Government' in the text box, and select **Magellan**, as shown below.

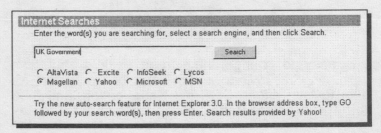

Clicking the **Search** button opens a Magellan search page, which is one of the many search utilities available for finding your way round the Web.

This searches the Web for references to the 'UK Government' and quickly opens a page of search results, the first few entries of which are shown below.

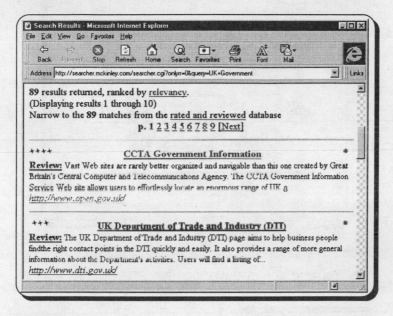

Magellan was aware of 89 relevant Web pages, and brought details of what it considered to be the ten most relevant ones to the screen. Search tools are very powerful and useful facilities, which we shall discuss more of in a later chapter.

In our case the first entry above will do. Clicking the blue underlined link CCTA Government Information will open the home page we were looking for, as shown on the next page.

If we had known the URL address (which is also given in the search details) we could have typed it straight into the **Address** slot, as follows:

```
http://www.open.gov.uk/
```

This would also have opened the same Web page when the Enter key on the keyboard was pressed.

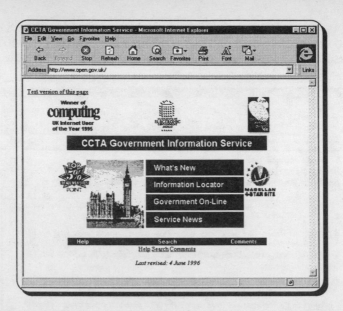

Quite a colourful display, but where is the menu?

Try moving the mouse pointer around the screen.

When it passes over some of the screen items it changes to a hand, as shown in our illustration.

That means each of these graphics is actually a link to another Web page. The status bar, at the bottom of the screen, shows the link as a 'Shortcut to..' the pointed to Web page. Clicking any of these links on the page will open another page, which may well contain more links.

We will leave it to you to explore this site further. You may find some interesting information, or on the other hand, it may help to send you to sleep.

NOTE - If a Web page is taking a long time to load you can open another browser window with the **File**, **New Window** command. You can have several Web pages open at the same time, all doing different things.

3. BASIC PROGRAM FEATURES

Explorer Screen Layout

The illustration below shows an empty Internet Explorer 3.0 window with the Toolbar maximised by dragging its bottom border down as far as it will go.

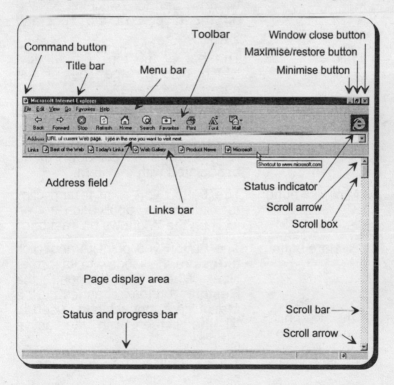

It is perhaps worth spending some time looking at the various parts that make up this window, which is subdivided into several areas with the following functions:

Area	*Function*
Command button	Clicking on this program icon button, located in the upper-left corner of each window, displays the pull-down Control menu which can be used to control the window. It includes commands for restoring, maximising, minimising, moving, sizing, and closing the window; and for switching on and off the display of the Tool and status bars.
Title bar	The bar at the top of a window which displays the title of the current Web page.
Menu bar	The bar below the title bar which allows you to choose from several menu options. Clicking on a menu item displays the pull-down menu associated with that item.
Minimise button	The button you point to and click to reduce an application to an icon on the Windows 95 Taskbar.
Restore button	The button you point to and click to restore the window to its former size. When that happens, the Restore button changes to a Maximise button which is used to fill the screen with the active window.
Close button	The X button that you click to close the window.
Toolbar	A bar of icons that you click to carry out some of the more common Explorer actions.

Address field	Shows the location of the current page, or the URL of the new page to go to next.
Links bar	These automatically load on-line Web pages and can be set up with your own favourite links.
Status indicator	Shows when data transfer is taking place.
Page display	The main body of the window that displays Web pages.
Scroll bars	If the contents of a window will not fit in it, scroll bars are added to the right and/or the bottom of the window.
Scroll arrows	The arrowheads at each end of a scroll bar which you can click to scroll the screen up and down, or left and right.
Scroll box	Dragging this box up or down the scroll bar will rapidly scroll through a Web page.
Status bar	The animated bar that shows the progress of a downloading operation and the address of the link or graphic, pointed to by the mouse.

At first glance an empty Explorer window looks a little grey and lifeless, but when you move the mouse pointer over the toolbar its buttons 'light up' when they are active. This is a very pleasing feature, the window being designed not to detract from the Web pages being viewed in it.

Menu Bar Options

Each option on the menu bar has associated with it a pull-down sub-menu. This follows the normal Windows convention, so to access the menu, either click the mouse on an option, or press the <Alt> key, which causes the first option of the menu (in this case **File**) to be highlighted, then use the arrow keys to highlight any of the options in the menu. Pressing either the <Enter> key, or the left mouse button, reveals the pull-down sub-menu of the highlighted menu option. The sub-menu of the **File** option is shown here.

Menu options can also be activated directly by pressing the <Alt> key followed by the underlined letter of the required option. Thus pressing **<Alt+F>**, also opens the sub-menu of **File**.

You can use the up and down arrow keys to move the highlighted bar up and down a sub-menu, or the right and left arrow keys to move along the options in the menu bar. Pressing the <Enter> key selects the highlighted option or executes the highlighted command. Pressing the <Esc> key once, closes the pull-down sub-menu, while pressing the <Esc> key for a second time, closes the menu system.

Note that those commands which are not available at any specific time will be inactive and appear on the menu in a lighter colour. In our example above the option **Save** is not available.

Keyboard Shortcuts:

Some of the menu options have keyboard shortcuts attached to them. These are very useful to people who are more used to the keyboard than the mouse. In the **File** sub-menu there are several. For example, pressing <Ctrl+N>, the 'N' key with the 'Ctrl' key also depressed, will open a new browser window.

We have listed the available shortcuts in Appendix A.

Mouse Right-Click Menu

You can use your right mouse button to click objects on a page and see a shortcut menu, with contents that depend on what you click:

On a link   The menu items refer to the page specified by the link.

On an image   They refer to the image file specified by the image.

On background They apply to the current page, its text, or its background image.

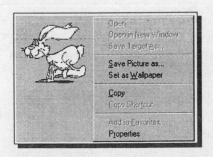

This example shows the options that were available when the mouse was right-clicked on the rabbit graphic image.

There were three main actions available; saving the picture to a disc file, setting it as the Windows wallpaper (heaven forbid), and copying the image to the clipboard. Clicking on **Properties** would show details of the image file.

As usual, unavailable options are shown in grey.

31

The Toolbar

Most Windows applications are now fully equipped with a Toolbar option, and Internet Explorer is no exception. It contains a series of buttons that you can click with your mouse pointer to quickly carry out a program function. The Mail and News windows also have their own Toolbars which are described later.

If the Toolbar is not showing when a window is opened, you simply open the **View** menu and select the **Toolbar** option. This places a tick '√' character on the sub-menu bar. Selecting it again in the future, will toggle the option off. You might want to remove the Toolbar so that you can view more data, or a whole picture, in the main page area.

The button functions are pretty self explanatory and are as follows:

Button	*Function*
Back	Displays the previous page in the history list.
Forward	Displays the next page in the history list.
Stop	Halts any on-line transfer of page data.
Refresh	Brings a fresh copy of the current Web page to the viewer.
Home	Displays your specified home page, with the Microsoft home page as the default.
Search	Opens an on-line page with access to search facilities.

Favorites Gives you quick access to your saved favourite sites, or bookmarks. This button is not necessary as it completely duplicates the **F̲avorites** menu option.

Print Prints the current Web page.

Font Steps the current page through four font sizes and re-displays the page each time. An excellent button.

Mail Gives access to Explorer's e-mail and Newsgroup facilities.

Layout of the Control Area:

If you find the Toolbar buttons a little on the large side you can change the way they appear on your screen, as well as the layout of the Address field and Links bar. This is very easily done by dragging the bottom frame of the Links bar up, or down, with the mouse pointer, as shown in the sequence below. The control area shrinks as you drag the frame up and expands again when it is dragged down.

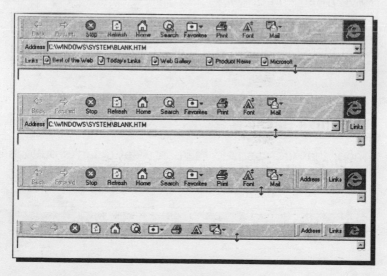

You can also try different combinations of controls in

the same bars by dragging the vertical lines as shown here.

This is really a very clever feature, which lets you drag the controls out of the way when you want to maximise the screen display area, without having to open the menu system at all.

The Address Field

The address field shows you the location (or URL address) of the current page being viewed. If you know the URL of the next page you want to look at, you can type it into this field.

Simply pressing the Enter key will load the page.

A pull-down menu, opened by clicking the down arrow at the right of the field, lets you choose from the most recent locations you have entered. This can save some typing!

The Links Bar

Under the Address field there is a set of Links buttons which, by default, open various on-line pages prepared for you by Microsoft and kept at their site.

These links are well worth exploring and may give you some ideas about where to go on the Web, and indeed, what can be usefully achieved instead of just surfing aimlessly from one link to another.

As an example, we show what was in the 'Best of the Web' page the last time we visited Microsoft's site. This will almost certainly have changed by the time this gets to you!

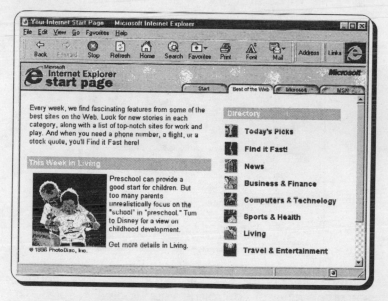

Each entry in the **Directory** list above is in fact a link to another Microsoft Web page. These give you 100s of links to explore (by clicking them with the mouse), and each one almost certainly has many more links built into it.

There is always something new, just over the horizon, on the Web.

The Links buttons do not have to stay pointing to Microsoft's pages. You can easily set them to hold your own most used sites, as is described in the next chapter.

General Option Settings

Like most Windows 95 programs, you control the way Internet Explorer operates for you, by changing settings in a series of tabbed dialogue boxes accessed with the **View**, **Options** menu command.

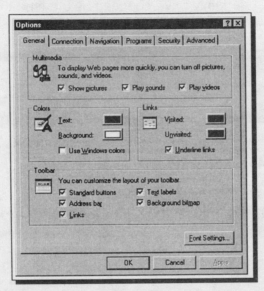

In the **General** tab sheet, shown open above, you will see other ways of controlling your Toolbar display. Try them out.

While you are at it, take a good look around the other options, both in this section and on the other tabbed sheets. If an option is not self explanatory, you can click the help button shown here (which is located in the top right of the window), then click the 'query' mouse pointer on the offending item to get more details of its function, as shown on the right.

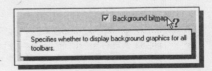

Saving Pictures

For many people, one of the big attractions of the Internet is the enormous collection of photographs and other graphical data that is freely available. Whatever your preferences, all you have to do is search until you find what you are looking for.

But how can I download a picture onto my PC and have it to look at, whenever I want? I hear you asking.

If you have followed this chapter up to this point you will not need to ask, you will probably be doing it already. If not, the procedure is very very easy. Once you have found the picture you want on a Web page, simply right-click your mouse on it and select from the object menu that opens.

Our example here, shows a graphic of an electronic navigation chart with the right-click menu options that are available. Clicking on **Save Picture as...** will open the Save As dialogue box for you to enter the **File name** and folder to **Save in** details. When you have done this, simply click the **Save** button to capture your picture. Don't fill up your hard disc though!

Explorer Help

The trend these days is for programs to be shipped with very little in the way of a manual and a much less detailed built-in Help system than was the norm a year or two ago. We shouldn't really complain about this as maybe that is why you are reading this book!

Internet Explorer only has a limited built-in Help system, which is accessed with the **Help**, **Help Topics** menu command. This opens a standard Windows 95 Help window, as shown below.

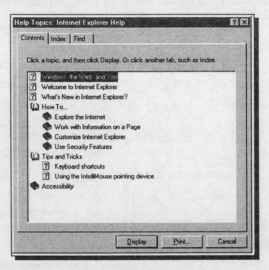

We strongly recommend that you work your way through all the listed items. Double-clicking on a closed book icon will open it and display a listing of its contents. Double-clicking on a list item will open a window with a few lines of Help information.

Another way of browsing the Help system is to click the **Index** tab and work your way through the alphabetic listing. The **Find** tab opens a search facility you can use. All in all we were not very impressed with the Browser Help provided by Microsoft. We would have expected some on-line detail of the program at least. Maybe that will come later!

There is a very basic on-line Web tutorial, accessed from the **Help** menu, with the **Web Tutorial** command, or from the first item in the above Help listing. This can, however, be very slow at times, depending on the amount of traffic crossing the Atlantic.

4. MORE SKILLS AND FEATURES

Some Starting Sites

As we saw in the last chapter, Microsoft have provided a starting page for your Web browsing. Hopefully you have launched out from this by now. If not, why not be cheeky and see what the oposition has to offer. With the launch of version 3.0 of the Navigator, Netscape have also designed a useful starting site for your Web travels that is opened by entering the following URL in the Address field, and pressing the <Enter> key.

```
http://home.netscape.com/escapes/index.html
```

This is, as you would expect from Netscape, a really professional page with point and click icons to other pages of suggested links.

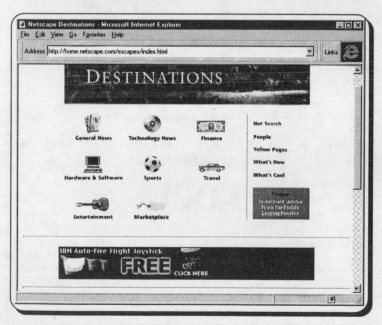

You can also see in our screen dump, an example of the almost garish advertising that is becoming more of a feature on many Web pages. The search engine pages also seem to be getting weighed down with it. Generating advertising revenue almost certainly helps to pay for some of our 'free' Web facilities, but at the expense of speed. Every graphic has to be downloaded and takes valuable time.

A Useful Site:

When you get fed up with surfing between sites which offer all manner of visual and audio entertainment, you might like to visit one useful page we recently found. Try entering the following address, which points to an American University site, so hopefully it will stay active. But don't forget things can change overnight on the Web.

`http://www.ithaca.edu/Library/Training/useful.html`

The header of this page is shown below. It is maintained by a librarian and points to an interesting array of reference and other kinds of library oriented sites.

ICYouSee:

What Can You Do On the WORLD WIDE WEB That Is Actually Useful?

Back to the ICYouSee Index?

One criticism of the Web is that it is just a big toy that is mostly good for wasting time. But mixed in with the strange and weird are some useful resources. Useful, I realize, can mean many things. For the purpose of this page, I'm limiting the definition of "useful" to "designed to promote research or support an academic curriculum." On this page I have tried to put together representative samples of some resources. The purpose is to be selective and illustrative, rather than exhaustive.

Using Web Information

Once you have found what you were looking for on the Web you can, with very little in the way of basic skills, save it to your own PC and use it for your own purposes. Every Web page consists of HTML code, text, graphic images, or links to files of some sort that have been used in the page construction. All of these can be saved, as we shall see.

The Mouse Pointer:

You have almost certainly noticed by now that the mouse pointer changes shape depending on what part of a page it is pointing to. There are three main shapes:

The main pointer which shows over inactive areas of a page. You cannot do anything in these areas.

The hand pointer that appears when you move over a link. Clicking the right mouse button opens a menu of actions you can carry out with that link, or its file.

The I beam pointer that means you can select the text beneath it.

Copying Text:

You can copy selected, or highlighted, text from an Explorer page to the Windows clipboard with the **Edit**, **Copy** menu command, or the <Ctrl+C> shortcut. If you want to copy all the text on a page, it is quicker to select it with the <Ctrl+A> keyboard shortcut, or the **Edit**, **Select All** command. The copied text will have all the HTML code stripped out.

Once the text you want is on the clipboard, you can **Paste** it into whatever open Windows application program you want, and then save it. Notepad is useful for this, or WordPad for a lot of text. But remember, the text might look formatted in WordPad, but this is only done with imported space characters.

Viewing Source Code:

If you want to see what the code for any page actually looks like, you can use the **View**, **Source** command. This opens the file in Notepad, so you can edit it as well. Our example below shows the actual HTML source code for the part of the Web page displayed in the illustration on page 40.

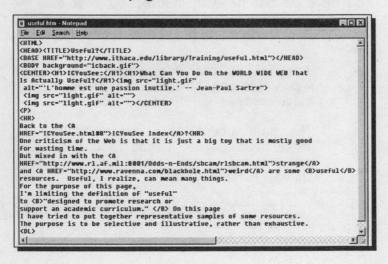

```
<HTML>
<HEAD><TITLE>Useful?</TITLE>
<BASE HREF="http://www.ithaca.edu/library/Training/useful.html"></HEAD>
<BODY background="icback.gif">
<CENTER><H1>ICYouSee:</H1><H1>What Can You Do On the WORLD WIDE WEB That
Is Actually Useful?</H1><img src="light.gif"
 alt="'L'homme est une passion inutile.' -- Jean-Paul Sartre">
 <img src="light.gif" alt="">
 <img src="light.gif" alt=""></CENTER>
<P>
<HR>
Back to the <A
HREF="ICYouSee.html#8">ICYouSee Index</A>?<HR>
One criticism of the Web is that it is just a big toy that is mostly good
for wasting time.
But mixed in with the <A
HREF="http://www.rl.af.mil:8001/Odds-n-Ends/sbcam/rlsbcam.html">strange</A>
and <A HREF="http://www.ravenna.com/blackhole.html">weird</A> are some <B>useful</B>
resources.  Useful, I realize, can mean many things.
For the purpose of this page,
I'm limiting the definition of "useful"
to <B>"designed to promote research or
support an academic curriculum." </B> On this page
I have tried to put together representative samples of some resources.
The purpose is to be selective and illustrative, rather than exhaustive.
<DL>
```

Saving a Whole Page:

The **File**, **Save As File** menu command lets you save the current Explorer page with all the HTML codes still in place. A page saved in this way does not retain its graphics, only the text and codes. Make sure, if you want to use the page again with your browser, that you save it with the default .htm extension.

There are several reasons for wanting to save a whole Web page to disc:

- So that you can edit the source code to form the basis of a page of your own.

- To create a hypertext 'reference book' of pages you have down-loaded. This would work on any PC that had the files on it.

- To use embedded links in a file as instant Bookmarks.

Saving a Target Link:

Explorer has another way of saving a Web file without you even having to open it. If you right-click your mouse pointer on a link in an open page, an object menu is opened, as we have seen before.

Selecting the **Save Target As** option from this menu, and completing the details of file name and destination folder in the Save As box, will start the download process. In our example above the ugly graphic was a link to a file available for downloading.

While the actual download is taking place a window like this is opened. This usually has a progress bar that indicates how the process is proceeding, and shows an estimate of the remaining time that will be taken.

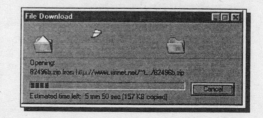

Downloading an Image Viewer

If you capture many graphics you may well need a program to view and manipulate them. One of the best shareware programs we have come across to do this is LView Pro, and as an example we will step you through the process of downloading this from the Internet.

To open the home page, shown below, type the following URL in the Address field and press <Enter>:

```
http://www.lview.com/
```

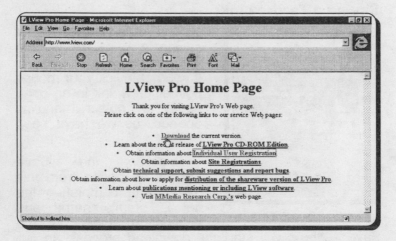

Clicking the <u>Download</u> link opens a page with very explicit details of how to download the program.

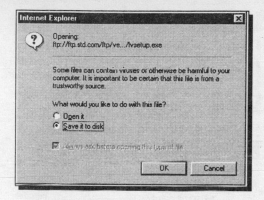

We suggest you open a new folder to receive it and then click the <u>here</u> link to start the process, which is in fact an FTP operation.

The warning box shown here is opened to make you aware that there is a danger of importing viruses if you download program files from an unknown source. The

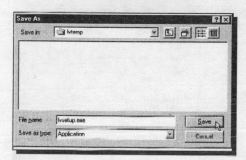

provider of this program should be a safe source, so make sure the **Save it to disk** option is selected and click the **OK** button.

Complete the details in the Save As dialogue box, as shown here, and click **Save** to start downloading. The File Download box is opened, but in our case, as shown below, Explorer could not find the size of the file so could give no progress details. No problem really, as long as this box is open the

downloading is still taking place. A flurry of disc activity and the closing of the File Download box will indicate the completion of the operation.

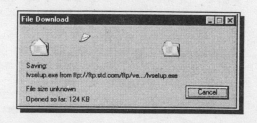

To check that the file has been received on your system, open the new **lvtemp** folder in a 'My Computer' window, and you should see it there as shown in our example on the left.

If you want to find out more about the file you could right-click the mouse pointer on its icon and select the **Properties** option from the opened menu.

This opens the tabbed dialogue box, shown below, which gives two pages of details about the file.

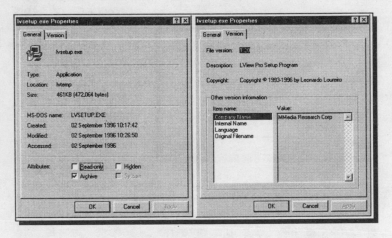

As you may well know, most objects in Windows 95 have properties, which you can examine and sometimes change in dialogue box panes like those above.

Once you have followed the on-line instructions and installed LView Pro you will have a very useful graphic utility program to evaluate. Of course, as it is shareware, if you carry on using it you should be prepared to pay the $30 registration fee.

Saving with Graphics

Although all the graphics and text code for a down-loaded Web page are actually saved in a cache on your hard disc you cannot simply copy these to another PC and view complete Web pages there. The link codings on the HTML page will not be correct. To save Explorer pages with their graphics embedded you need extra software to sort out this problem.

Many sites on the Web specialise in providing software for all sorts of special applications. One of our favourites is called Tucows, shown below, which you can reach with the following URL address:

http://www.ukonline.co.uk/tucows/index.html

They have hundreds of Windows shareware and demonstration programs available for you to download and use. It is a very good way of testing and evaluating a program, before parting with your money.

Printing Web Pages

It was originally thought by some, that computers would lead to the paper-less office. That has certainly not proved to be correct. It seems that however good our electronic communication media becomes most people want to see the results printed on paper. As far as books are concerned, long may that last!

Microsoft have built into their Explorer the ability to produce very good printed output of Web pages. The screen layout of an Explorer page depends on the size of the window you have open and the font size you are using. Try this out by viewing a page full screen and then reducing it to a smaller window. The page will be re-formatted around any embedded graphics. The same thing happens when you print, except that the paper size, not the window, determines the eventual layout.

Before you print, you should check the page settings with the **File**, **Page Setup** command. When you are ready, click the Print button, or use the <Ctrl+P> key combination, or the **File**, **Print** menu command, to open the Print dialogue box shown here.

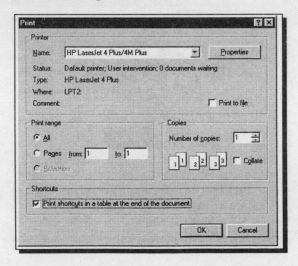

Make sure the correct printer is selected, choose the pages to be printed, and how many copies, and finally click **OK** to start the printing process. You should be impressed with the results, especially if you have a high resolution laser printer.

A very useful feature in the above dialogue box, that we have not yet seen elsewhere, is the ability to **Print shortcuts in a table at the end of a document**.

When this option is checked, you get a hardcopy listing of the URL addresses of all the links present in the printed Web page.

Your Own Home, or Start, Page

When you browse the World Wide Web you'll see the term 'home page' used quite a lot. This is usually the starting point, or start page, of a Web site, which gives an overview of what you'll find there.

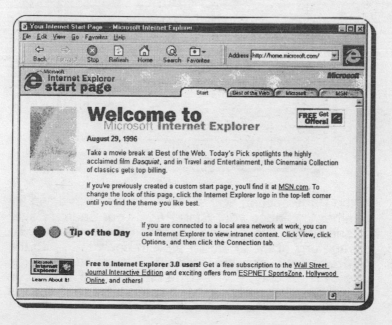

Your own home page is the Web page that the Explorer automatically opens when you first switch on. By default, your browser is set to open at Microsoft's own home page site, shown on the previous page. This may be useful the first few times, and of course gives them lots of advertising space, but you will soon want to change it.

This, like most things with the Explorer, is quite easy to do. You control what you want as your home page in the settings sheet opened with the **View**, **Options**, menu command and then clicking the **Navigation** tab.

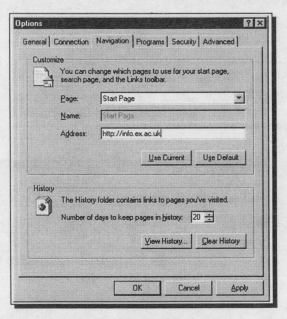

In the **Page** section you select from the drop-down list whether to change your Start Page, your Search Page, or one of the five named pages on the Links bar. To change any of these, either type the new URL into the **Address** field, or with the new page open, click the **Use Current** button. The page can even be located on your hard disc, but must be an HTM file that is readable by the Explorer.

Some Ideas for a Home Page:

- Some people make up their own home page of data and links to their favourite starting points.

- Others use one of the many search engine pages available on the Web. Unless you use a local one, though, this can sometimes be slow.

- If you are connected to a company, or work, network they should have a home page that can show useful internal information and links.

- You can usually use your Internet provider's own home page.

- Simply use a Web page that displays your favourite pictures, or plays your favourite music, to inspire you to get to work!

A Custom Home Page:

Microsoft make it fairly easy for you to build an active home, or start, page of your own at the site opened by the following URL address and shown on the facing page.

```
http://www.msn.com
```

In fact at the time of writing, there is a link to this Microsoft Network (MSN) site from the Microsoft home page shown on page 49.

Whether you use this is up to you, but it is there. Once you have your own home page, just remember that wherever you are on the Web you can always return to it by clicking the **Home** Toolbar icon.

History Files

The Explorer keeps track of all the Web pages and files you view, and stores them in the **windows/history** folder. To see this, you can open the History window with the <u>Go</u>, **Open <u>H</u>istory Folder** menu option. It will look something like that shown below.

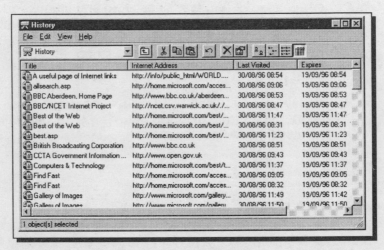

In this window you can scroll through the sites you have recently visited, and double-clicking a **Title** will re-open that Web page in the browser.

Some of this History information is also added to the <u>Go</u> menu. Just clicking one of these items will open that Web page.

You can control the length of time that the Explorer keeps this History information in the settings sheet that is opened with the **<u>V</u>iew**, **<u>O</u>ptions**, menu command and then clicking the **Navigation** tab, as shown on page 50.

Ours was set for the default 20 days, which is also shown in the above History information, where all the files expire 20 days after they were last visited. You can delete them by clicking the **<u>C</u>lear History** button.

The Cache

You may have noticed that a Web page, especially one with lots of graphics, loads more quickly into Explorer if you have already recently viewed it. This is because all the pages and files you view are stored in a temporary cache on your hard disc. The next time you access that page, depending on your settings, Explorer checks to see if the page has been updated before bringing it from the cache. If any change to the page has occurred, the new version is downloaded. If not, a cached copy is quickly retrieved.

Some Web pages, that are frequently updated, tell you to clear your cache before going any further. You do this, and generally control the cache, from the Options box shown below, which is opened with the **View**, **Options** command and pressing the **Advanced** tab.

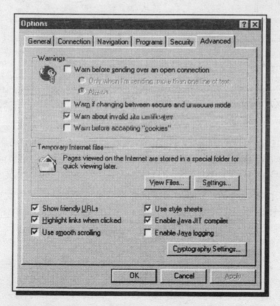

Press **View Files** to open the Temporary Internet Files folder, or **Settings** to open the following control box.

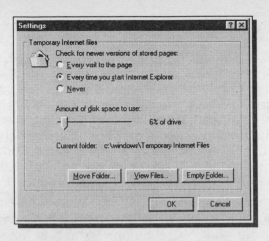

This shows that, in our case, these temporary files are stored in a cache in the C:\windows\Temporary Internet Files folder, and that Web sites are checked for changes only the first time they are accessed in every Explorer session. If you leave your PC running for any length of time, you may want to change this setting to check **Every visit to the page,** but page loading will be a little slower.

Pressing the **Empty Folder** button will clear the cache, which will very rapidly free up space on your hard disc.

If you are short of space on your hard disc, you can reduce the size of your cache by lowering the **Amount of disk space to use** slider. Again this will reduce the number of sites that can be cached, and may slow you down. If you have another hard disc you could also move the cache onto it by clicking the **Move Folder** button.

Security

Because of its design the Internet does not provide security for any data transmitted across it. As we saw in Chapter 1, data travelling between your computer and a server somewhere else in the World passes through a large number of computer systems. An operator at any one of these computers has the potential to view, manipulate, or even corrupt, your data, which can thus be very susceptible to fraud or other misuse by unscrupulous individuals.

For most casual Web browsing this would not really matter, but if you are conducting business, or sending sensitive information, such as details of your credit card, you need security measures to make sure that your data is safe.

Explorer Security Measures:

Netscape Communications originally developed a security technology called SSL, (short for Secure Sockets Layer protocol), which has become a standard since it was put into the public domain for the Internet community. This SSL protocol checks the identity of the server being accessed, carries out data encryption of any messages sent, and guarantees their general integrity. SSL is layered beneath the Internet application protocols (HTTP, Telnet, FTP, Gopher, etc.), but above the TCP/IP connection protocol. In this way it operates independently of the Internet protocols.

Microsoft Explorer supports SSL 2.0 and 3.0, as well as PCT 1.0 (Private Communication Technology), which enable you to make secure credit-card purchases from a Web page. With these active on both your browser and the server you are transmitting to, your sensitive communications should be absolutely secure and unusable by third parties.

With Explorer you can tell whether a page, or document comes from a secure server protected by

SSL, by looking at the address (URL) field. If the URL begins with https:// (instead of http://), it is from a secure server.

A Secure Transaction:

As an example of a typical secure transaction carried out with Internet Explorer version 3.0, we will step through the process of registering our copy of the shareware program LView Pro which we downloaded earlier in the chapter.

From the LView Pro home page, shown on page 44, clicking the *Individual User Registration* link opens a page similar to that shown here.

LView Pro Individual User Registration

Thank you for your interest in registering LView Pro. We offer the following options of registration:

- LView Pro CD-ROM Edition (US$40 within USA, US$48 outside USA):
- 1.44 disk (US$35 within USA, US$42 outside USA):
- Email delivery (US$30 worldwide):
  User name and id# are delivered by email, software and help file are downloaded from an on-line service.
  For more information about downloading the software, please click here

To register LView Pro on-line, when paying with a **credit card**:

- If using an SSL Web browser such as Netscape or Microsoft Explorer, please click here to access a secure document.
- If using another Web browser, please click here.

The above part page shows a link to the site's secure application form, with the hand pointer over it. The address of the linked site is displayed in the status bar,

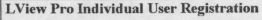

as shown below. This points to a '(secure Web site)'.

- If using an SSL Web browser such as Netscape or Microsoft Explorer, please click here to access a secure document.

Shortcut to iregform.htm at commerce.mindspring.com (secure Web site)

Clicking the *here* link opens the secure Web page shown on our next page. Note the 's' in the https:// part of the URL in the Address field, and the padlock security indicator on the status bar, both showing that the transaction will be secure.

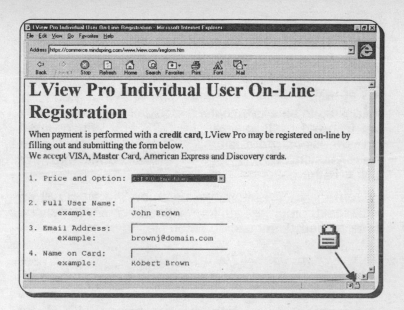

If you carry on and complete the form with your credit card and other personal details when you send it you can be confident that your details will not be intercepted. You must, of course, be happy that your details will be treated correctly at the other end. But that is the same with any transaction.

Netscape Plug-in Support

To make sure that you can use all the Web page content available on the Internet, Explorer 3.0 is compatible with Netscape's proprietary Plug-in technology, as well as with ActiveX Controls. This means that if you open a site that expects a plug-in, Explorer checks to see if it is installed. If not, a page is automatically opened for you where either the Plug-in or an equivalent ActiveX control can be downloaded.

More detail on these features is really outside the scope of this book.

Different File Formats

While exploring the Web, you will encounter many different types of files and file formats. The way to tell the format of a file, and hence find out what it does, is to look at its extension, which is usually expressed as a dot followed by 2 to 4 letters. DOS and Windows 3.1 file extensions were limited to three characters, so a file extension with four letters is usually a Macintosh or UNIX file format.

Most of the files you encounter on the Web will be either text, graphics, audio or video files; some may be compressed. The most common files to be found are:

Compressed
With extensions like .ZIP, .SIT and .TAR.

Graphics
With the extensions .JPEG (or .JPG), a popular compression file standard for photograph quality images; and .GIF, an older format developed by CompuServe in the late 1980s.

Video
With the popular extensions of .AVI, .MPG, .MOV.

Sound
Files come in .AIFF (for the Mac). .AU for the Mac and UNIX. .WAV for the PC, and .RA (Real Audio) a new proprietary system for delivering and playing real-time audio on the Web.

You may need to be able to identify these and other file types before you can use them, so we have included an Appendix of the main file formats at the back of this book.

5. WHERE SHALL WE GO TODAY?

For anyone not involved with the World Wide Web, Microsoft's advertising catch phrase "Where do you want to go today?" is probably a bit confusing. For those of us that do a little surfing the confusion is, how do we choose where to go?

You can literally spend hours following links from one place to another, and at the end of the day sometimes getting nowhere useful. But if you want some specific information you will have to use one, or more, of the many search engines that are available.

Finding the Search Tools

There are a number of search tools, or engines, available to help you find what you want on the Web. Some search all the contents of documents, others only the file name. Most of them rank the search results in order depending on the number of times the searched for words appear in a document.

Basically there are two types:

- Tools like **Yahoo**, **Magellan** and **Excite** search for Web sites, so are best used for searching by broad subject areas. They will find sites that generally cover the subject you are searching for.

- Search engines like **Alta Vista**, **Lycos** and **WebCrawler** will find individual pages of a Web site that match your search, even if the site itself has nothing to do with what you are looking for.

Each search tool seems to use a different method of searching, so your search results may vary when you use different ones. Be patient as you may not always find what you're looking for very easily.

Search

At the end of Chapter 2 we saw that the easy way to find a search tool is to click the **Search** Toolbar button. Otherwise you can use the **Help**, **Microsoft on the Web**, **Search the Web** menu command sequence. They both open a page, part of which is shown below, which gives you access to some of the main Search tools that are available, but more seem to be added to the Web all the time.

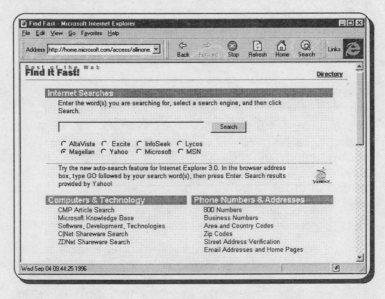

Below the search tool section are some tabulated search links which eventually lead to many sites which may well be of interest. At the moment these seem to be mostly relevant to the US, but not all. A novel feature of this window is the clock on the status bar.

Yahoo, one of the search tool operators, have formed a special link with Microsoft. You can carry out a rapid Yahoo search by typing GO followed by your search word(s), in the Address field and then pressing the <Enter> key.

What is Available

In the next few pages we alphabetically list the main search tools that are available to you, with their URL addresses and a few comments on each. Be patient with them, they are all different. With most you simply type in the text you want to search for, but they usually offer much more complicated searches as well. If you have problems, look for a Help link and spend a few minutes reading how best to use the site's facilities.

A2Z

`http://a2z.lycos.com/`

The Lycos A2Z directory starts with the most frequently linked sites, and adds concise, authoritative descriptions.

ACCUFIND

`http://nln.com/`

This JavaScript search engine automatically searches infobases, news, books, and the Internet.

AIRS II

`http://www.arachnae.com/UofT.html`

Using easy Boolean and fuzzy queries, AIRS II's full-text search services have been used by large corporations, and now you can use those same services to find exactly what you are seeking.

ALTA VISTA

`http://altavista.digital.com/`

A product of Digital Equipment Corporation (DEC), this creates complete indexes of every word on every Web page or Usenet newsgroup it encounters, allowing you to make highly targeted searches. Alta Vista allows simple and advanced searches and can help you find your way through the 8 billion words in 30 million Web pages. It also provides a full-text index of more than 13,000 newsgroups.

AMAZING ENVIRONMENTAL ORGANIZATION WEBDIRECTORY!

`http://www.webdirectory.com/`

The categories in this environmental Web directory cover topics such as animal rights, solar energy, and sustainable development.

ARGUS/UNIVERSITY OF MICHIGAN CLEARING HOUSE

`http://www.lib.umich.edu/chhome.html`

The Clearinghouse has provided access to topical guides to the Internet's information since 1993. Hundreds of topics, from artificial intelligence to zoology, are available. Searchable and browsable, it also includes guide ratings.

C|NET'S SHAREWARE.COM

`http://www.shareware.com/`

This tool makes it simple to find software on the Internet. More than 170,000 files are available for easy searching, browsing, and down-loading from shareware and corporate archives.

DEJANEWS

`http://www.dejanews.com/`

A specialist tool that searches Usenet newsgroups, and cuts through the millions of postings with absolute ease. See an example of how it works at the end of the chapter.

THE ELECTRIC LIBRARY

`http://www.elibrary.com/id/2525`

Rather than searching the Web, check out the Electric Library's contents. Launch comprehensive searches across this extensive database of more than 1,000 full-text newspapers, magazines, academic journals, images, reference books, literature, and art.

EXCITE

http://www.excite.com/

Offers two different ways to search: by keyword and by concept. Its concept-based searches allow you to search based on what you mean and not just what you say, by using plain English search 'phrases'. It places an icon next to each result allowing you to view more documents of a similar nature. Excite also allows you to view results in different modes. Excite's Web index covers the full text of 11.5 million pages and is updated weekly. Reviews are available of 55,000 sites, plus Usenet newsgroups, hourly news, commentary, and the Web's first interactive cartoon!

GAMELAN

http://www.gamelan.com/

A central repository for Java applications, sorted by category.

GNN SELECT

http://gnn.com/gnn/wic/wics/index.html

GNN's own surfers choose and review the Net's best sites and programs, from Activism and Adventure Travel to Women's Studies and Zines.

G.O.D.

http://www.god.co.uk/

Europe's premier search tool using a unique global filter, or categorised site listings, it includes free online classified ads or you can add your own site instantly.

HOTBOT

`http://www.hotbot.com/`

A search engine capable of indexing the entire World Wide Web, every week. HotBot's next-generation interface lets you search on Java, VRML, and Netscape plug-ins, and allows you to limit searches by date, domain, or continent.

IBM INFOMARKET

`http://www.infomarket.ibm.com/`

Allows the 'serious user', in other words 'one with money', to simultaneously search Web and commercial resources including 66 newswires, 300 newspapers, 770 newsletters, 6,300 journals and 11.5 million company details. Information can be purchased on a per document basis using IBM's Cryptolope technology, enabling users to buy and sell content securely over the Internet.

INFOSEEK GUIDE

`http://guide.infoseek.com/Home`

With each search, you get the most relevant matches, related topics to explore, and timely news and views from popular magazines, TV networks, and the best on-line experts. Infoseek Guide also makes it easy to find e-mail addresses, stock quotes, company profiles, and more.

LYCOS

`http://a2z.lycos.com/`

Lycos software robots actually go out and travel the Internet every day looking for new Web, Gopher and FTP sites. All new sites are included in the Lycos database. It can be somewhat awkward to use, but it does the most thorough search.

MAGELLAN

http://www.mckinley.com/

Developed by The McKinley Group, a publisher of print directories. Over 40,000 of the Web sites in its index have been reviewed and rated by their editorial staff. Magellan lets you navigate the Internet and preview content. You do a keyword search and are presented with a list of results each of which is described in a one paragraph summary and rated according to a four-star rating system. If you want to read a comprehensive review of the site, click on the Summary link. The number of stars tells you how good the site is, based on completeness of coverage, organisation, age, and ease of access.

NERD WORLD MEDIA INTERNET SUBJECT INDEX

http://www.nerdworld.com/

Search thousands of categories for the exact Web site or newsgroup that you're looking for. Check out the Make-Your-Own-Index feature and the pop-up search page.

100HOT WEBSITES

http://www.100hot.com/

Lists the most popular sites every week. Find the hottest Web sites in the hottest categories: live events, technology, models, celebrities, humour, showbiz. 100hot is like the best-seller list, but for Web sites, by country. This is a good place to come if you are a little bored!

OPEN TEXT INDEX

http://www.opentext.com/omw/f-omw.html

Searches every word of every Web page the company has indexed - some 21 billion words and phrases in all. It is claimed to be one of the largest indexes available.

POINT

`http://www.pointcom.com/`

Search an extensive database of rated and reviewed Web sites and check out Point's cream of the cybercrop - sites their editors place in the top five percent. Also offers a weekly Top Ten list and international news headlines.

THE SOFTWARE SHARING RESOURCE LIBRARY

`http://ssrl.rtp.com:443/Harvest/brokers/reuse/query`

This resource sponsors a special program to find and reward Web sites that offer free software or shareware, resulting in a database of PC and Unix tools, as well as a general index of Web sites.

STARTING POINT

`http://www.stpt.com/`

Use Starting Point to browse the Web, in categories such as news, business, sports, and entertainment.

WEBCRAWLER

`http://www.webcrawler.com/`

This popular site offers a speedy Web search engine and a random-links feature to find new and unusual sites. WebCrawler searches the contents of pages within a site, for a match with the search terms you entered, even if the site itself is unrelated to what you are searching for. It also features a list of the 25 most visited sites on the Web.

W3 SERVERS

`http://www.w3.org/pub/DataSources/WWW/Servers.html`

This directory at the World Wide Web Consortium lists registered Web servers around the world.

WHAT'S NEW

`http://www.emap.com/whatsnew/`

A list of the best new sites on the Web, updated daily.

WHOWHERE?

`http://www.whowhere.com/`

A comprehensive White Pages service for locating people and organisations on the Net. It intuitively handles misspelled or incomplete names, and it lets you search by initials.

WORLD WIDE WEB WORM

`http://wwww.cs.colorado.edu/wwww`

Builds its index based on Web page titles and URL contents only. This is less inclusive, especially if poor page titles have originally been used, but the pages it finds are more likely to be an exact match with your request.

YAHOO

`http://www.yahoo.com/`

Probably the pioneer Internet guide, which has recently developed a special link with Microsoft. Yahoo is one of the most popular hierarchical indexes of Web sites by subject. You can search the index by subject, or specify a search term. Yahoo is good if you're searching for general information on a subject, but because of the way information is indexed, if you're looking for something specific, you probably won't get the best results with it. It is updated daily and gives up-to-the-minute sports scores, weather, headlines, and stock quotes - though mostly American of course.

If you can't find what you are looking for with one of these search tools then it may well not exist. Happy searching.

DEJANEWS - As an Example

We cannot include examples of all the search tools listed, but to give you an idea of their power we have dabbled with a DEJANEWS search. For anyone starting to get to grips with the Usenet newsgroups this tool is essential.

As we saw earlier, the address of the Dejanews site is:

`http://www.dejanews.com/`

This opens the Web page shown below, complete with colourful advertising, which seems to be a feature of most search pages now. I guess it helps keep the searches free to the rest of us.

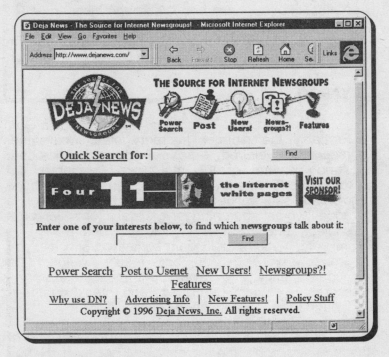

This has a box for you to enter the text of a quick, or simple, search.

Clicking the **Features** icon will open details of the News features offered and how to use them.

We are interested in sailing and generally finding our way round the oceans, so we entered **Navigation** in the **Quick Search for:** box and then pressed **Find**. The search results are shown below.

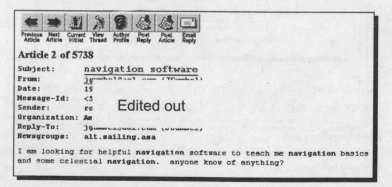

Hits 1-20 of 5738 for Query: **Navigation**

	Date	Scr	Subject	Newsgroup	Author
1.	96/09/04	027	Re: Sexant navigation in	alt.sailing.asa	"Unc"
2.	96/09/02	027	navigation software	alt.sailing.asa	jgm
3.	96/09/04	026	Re: Forms 4.5 and mouse	comp.databases.orac	sim
4.	96/09/04	026	Re: Russian TU-154 down	alt.disasters.aviat	"T.
5.	96/09/03	026	Re: Aggregate Navigation	comp.databases.syba	Jo
6.	96/09/03	026	Re: Agent · Í '°¼° ° °í ³	han.comp.internet	bla
7.	96/09/03	026	US-CA-Palmdale, Lockheed	la.jobs	csi
8.	96/09/03	026	>> Great Circle Navigat	aus.aviation	c94
9.	96/09/03	025	?? Cruise Missles using	sci.geo.satellite-n	jne
10.	96/09/03	025	Re: Ver 1.2 on an XT - k	comp.os.geos	dki
11.	96/09/03	025	Re: Mimicking GPS satell	sci.geo.satellite-n	"J.
12.	96/09/08	013	Flip Wilson	alt.showbiz.gossip	bas
13.	96/09/02	025	Aggregate Navigation	comp.databases.syba	Ott
14.	96/09/02	025	Re: HELP: directory tree	comp.infosystems.ww	And
15.	96/09/02	025	Wanted Sextant navigatio	alt.sailing.asa	loc
16.	96/08/31	025	Re: Ver 1.2 on an XT - keybo	comp.os.geos	fig
17.	96/08/31	025	HELP: directory tree nav	comp.infosystems.ww	muc
18.	96/08/31	024	Re: Transatlanic Navigat	rec.aviation.simula	pat
19.	96/08/31	024	Re: Ver 1.2 on an XT - k	comp.os.geos	gus
20.	96/08/31	024	GPS navigation system	rec.boats	Joh

Edited out

Get next 20 hits

This showed us that navigation was a popular word among the Usenet users. All of the underlined entries above are active links to news articles that have been posted, or to their authors. We clicked the subject link for article 2 and read the posting, some of which is shown slightly amended below.

Previous Article | Next Article | Current Hitlist | View Thread | Author Profile | Post Reply | Post. Article | Email Reply

Article 2 of 5738

Subject:	navigation software
From:	jg_____@___ ___ (_____)
Date:	19
Message-Id:	<5
Sender:	ro
Organization:	An
Reply-To:	jg_____ (_____)
Newsgroups:	alt.sailing.asa

Edited out

I am looking for helpful **navigation** software to teach me **navigation** basics and some celestial **navigation**. anyone know of anything?

Probably the content is not of much interest to many people in itself, but it's the principle we are trying to get over. At the top of this message page is a series of menu buttons which are worth looking at.

With the **Previous Article** and **Next Article** options you can work your way through the other messages in the retrieved listing and pressing **Current Hitlist** will return you to it. **View Thread** will locate any other messages in the same series, so that you can follow the whole 'conversation'.

The **Post Reply** and **Post Article** graphic menu options let you actually compose and send your own messages to the Usenet group, and **Email Reply** lets you send a personal message to the author, all without even leaving Dejanews.

Clicking **Author Profile** opens a page showing details of every message the writer of the current article has sent to the Usenet groups, as shown in the edited example below. This may help you assess the value of an article by showing you the writer's 'history'.

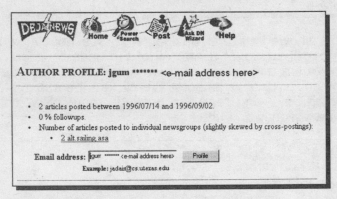

You can also use Dejanews to open, read and communicate with, your regular newsgroups. A useful facility, if you have problems with the Explorer Newsreader. In all, a very powerful facility, which at the moment is free of charge. Let's hope it stays that way!

6. USING FAVORITES

Using Favorites, which are Microsoft's version of Bookmarks (their spelling not ours!) is an easy way to access the Web pages that you need to visit on a regular basis. It is much easier to select a page URL address from a sorted list, than to look it up and manually type it into the Address field.

The Favorites Menu

With the Internet Explorer, a Favorite is simply a Windows 95 short cut to a Web page that the program places in the windows\favorites folder. When you first use Explorer there will be no Favorites available. Later, as your list of regular sites grows, your Favorites menu structure will grow too.

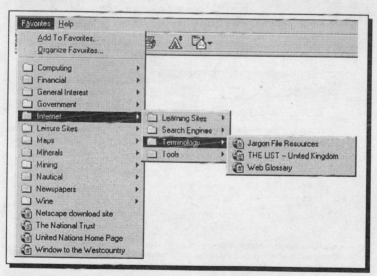

The illustration above shows the menu that opens when the **Favorites** menu option is actioned on one of our PCs. When the Explorer was first loaded, only the first two control items were present on this menu. We

71

have added the others and organised them in folders. In fact only a few items in the main and right-hand menus are Favorites, or short cuts, the others consist of a hierarchy of folders that contain relevant Favorites.

Adding a Favorite:

There are several ways to add a Favorite to the menu. When you are viewing a Web page that you want to visit again, the easiest method is to right-click on the page and select **Add to Favorites** from the object menu. The **Favorites**, **Add to Favorites** menu command will also start the procedure. They both open the Add to Favorites box shown below.

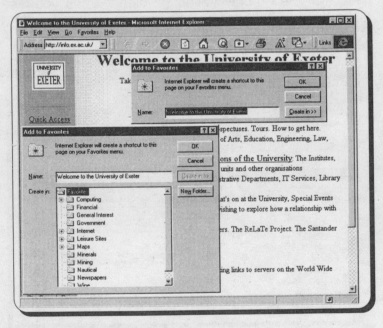

This composite shows several stages at once. We are adding the Welcome... Web page to our list. Clicking the **Create in** button opens the other part of the box, for you to select a folder to receive the Favorite. Clicking the **OK** button will complete the process.

You could also simply click the first **OK** button to add the new Favorite to the bottom of the list. It would then appear at the bottom of the **Favorites** menu. Each time you add a Web page like this, the page's title is offered as the menu item.

The next time you open the Favorites menu that item should be there for you to use.

Using Favorites:

To open a Web page pointed to by a Favorite, you simply open the **Favorites** menu and click the item's name in the drop-down menu.

The Organize Favorites Window

You won't have to visit many pages before your Favorites menu will get very full and difficult to use. It is then time to tidy up a little.

You choose the **Favorites**, **Organize Favorites** command to open a window in which you can easily organise your Favorites, as shown below.

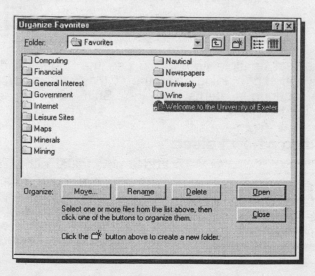

The window contains both Favorite icons and folders to store them in, which can be nested in other folders to produce a hierarchical, or multilevel, menu. It has its own menu buttons to manipulate and maintain your Favorites as you want. If you are happy handling files and folders in Windows 95 by dragging them around a window you will not need these buttons. You can do the same in this window.

Selecting Items:

Double-clicking on a folder icon will display or hide its contents. Single-clicking on a Favorite icon, or folder, will select (or deselect) it, so that you can **Move**, **Delete**, or **Rename** it. Remember that actions carried out on a folder also affect the contents of that folder. If you delete a folder you will lose all its contents as well! But you do get the option to cancel.

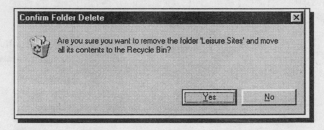

To select multiple items, you use the usual Windows convention of holding down the <Ctrl> key and clicking non-contiguous items, or the Shift key to select contiguous ones.

Adding a New Folder:

To add a new folder either, click the Create New Folder toolbar button, as shown here, or right-click in the empty window space and select **New**, **Folder** from the opened object menus.

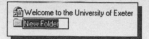

Both of these place a new folder at the end of the existing list box shown here. Type the new folder name and press the <Enter> key. You can then drag any of your existing Favorites into this folder, or nest folders by simply dragging one into another.

Favorite Properties

Every Favorite has a set of properties which you can edit quite easily from the Properties box.

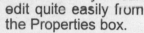

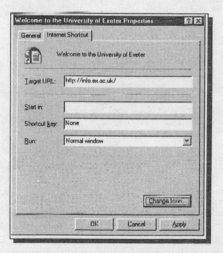

The easiest way to open this box is to right-click on your Favorite and select **Properties** from the menu.

You can change the **Target URL** of the page, set a **Shortcut key** to open it, or set the type of window it is **Run** in. The **Change Icon** button lets you customise it further.

The **General** tab opens another section which shows the Favorite file details and the date and time that it was created, modified and last accessed.

We will leave it up to you to explore the further possibilities here. As soon as anyone publishes a page on the Web you have the capability of downloading any of its features to your PC, and using them yourself. Be careful of any copyright infringements though.

7. E-MAIL

The Internet Explorer 3.0 has a very powerful mail facility built into it, which now makes it very easy for you to send and receive e-mail messages. We were so impressed with this part of the program that we now use it for all our e-mail correspondence.

What is E-mail

E-mail, or electronic mail, is cheaper, quicker, and usually much easier to prepare and send than Post Office mail. So what is an e-mail? It's simply an electronic message sent between computers which can include attachments like pictures, document files or even Web pages. The message is passed from one computer to another as it travels through the Internet, with each computer reading its e-mail address and routing it further until it reaches its destination, where it is stored in a 'mailbox'. This usually only takes a few minutes, and sometimes only seconds.

You can use e-mail for keeping in touch with friends and family and for professional reasons. You can send e-mail to most people, anywhere in the world, as long as they have their own e-mail address. These days all Internet service providers offer an e-mail address and mailbox facility to all their customers.

To retrieve your e-mail messages you have to contact your mailbox, download them to your PC, and then read and process them (just like any other mail).

As we shall see, Explorer 3.0 makes this whole procedure very easy and takes most of the mystery out of the whole e-mail process.

E-mail Addresses:

An e-mail address usually has two main parts, which are separated with the '@' character, and usually contain at least one dot (the '.' character). The following is a typical, if short, example.

aperson@organisation.co.uk

The part before the @ is the user name which identifies him, or her, at the mailbox. This user name is usually made up from the name and initials of the user.

After the @ comes the domain name, which identifies the computer where the person has a mailbox and is usually the name of a company, a university, or other organisation. There is a central register of these domain names, as each must be unique. When you set up your account, you can sometimes get your service provider to customise a domain name for you, at a price, of course. Otherwise you will probably use the domain name of the service provider itself.

Next, there's a '.' or dot, followed by two, or three, letters that indicate the type of domain it is. In our example above this is **.co** which means the host is a business or commercial enterprise, located in the United Kingdom (**.uk**). In the USA this would be **.com** instead, but not followed by a country identifier.

A host name ending with **.edu** means the host is a US university or educational facility. A UK university would be **.ac.uk**. A **.org** indicates the host is a US non-commercial organisation.

Some of the more common extensions you might encounter are:

edu	Educational sites in the US
com	Commercial sites in the US
gov	Government sites in the US
net	Network administrative organisations

mil	Military sites in the US
org	Organisations in the US that don't fit into other categories
fr	France
ca	Canada
uk	United Kingdom
**	Other county codes

Once you get used to these address parts, they begin to make more sense. For example, the writer's e-mail address is

poliver@csm.ex.ac.uk

This reads quite easily as:

P. Oliver located at Camborne School of Mines, part of the University of Exeter, which is an academic institution in the UK.

So if you know where somebody works you can even make an attempt to guess his, or her, e-mail address. A home address obtained through a commercial Internet provider would not be very easy though.

Finding an E-mail Address:

The **Search** button on the Explorer Toolbar gives easy access to an e-mail address directory site, as shown here.

Phone Numbers & Addresses
800 Numbers
Business Numbers
Area and Country Codes
Zip Codes
Street Address Verification
Email Addresses and Home Pages

We clicked the 'Email Addresses and Home Pages' link and entered the writer's own details in the search box shown on the next page.

79

This shows that the facility being used is the FOUR11 White Page Directory, which is one of many e-mail directories available on the Web.

We did not really expect to get a positive search result, but were surprised to find 17 Phil Olivers in the directory.

```
SUCCESSFUL SEARCH, MATCHES: 17 (click on listings for additional details)

GIVEN NAMES      FAMILY NAME      E-MAIL DOMAIN
---------------  ---------------  -----------------------
Phil             Oliver           @GUILDPRESS.COM
Phil             Oliver           @INDY.NET
PHILIP DANIEL    OLIVER           @iastate.edu
Philip R         Oliver           @csm.ex.ac.uk
```

Clicking on the bottom one of those listed above gave the following quite complete personal details.

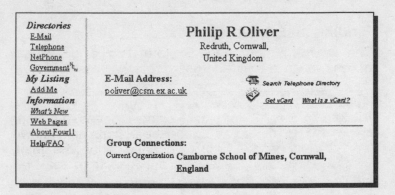

Directories
E-Mail
Telephone
NetPhone
Government

My Listing
Add Me

Information
What's New
Web Pages
About Four11
Help/FAQ

Philip R Oliver

Redruth, Cornwall,
United Kingdom

E-Mail Address:
poliver@csm.ex.ac.uk

Search Telephone Directory

Get vCard   What is a vCard?

Group Connections:
Current Organization **Camborne School of Mines, Cornwall, England**

If you don't find your details here, you can click the Add Me link to remedy the situation. These e-mail directories are getting more detailed all the time.

Using Microsoft Mail

To start the Mail program, click the **Mail** Explorer Toolbar icon and then select **Read Mail** from the menu that opens, as shown on the left.

Before you can use your browser to send, or receive, mail you have to tell the program how to connect to your server's facilities. You can do this in two ways. By completing your personal e-mail connection details in the Internet Mail Configuration Wizard, which opens when you first attempt to use the Mail program.

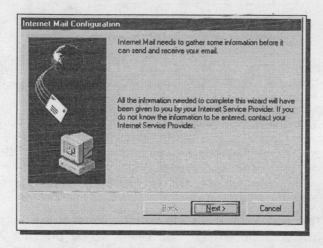

The other way, if the Mail window opens but your details are not correct, is to use the options box, shown on the next page, which is opened when the **Mail**, **Options**, menu command is actioned from the Mail window, and the **Server** tab is clicked.

To complete the details in this box you may need to ask your Internet service provider or system administrator for your details. The ones shown here will obviously only work for the writer, so don't try them!

81

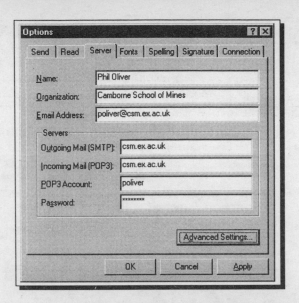

You type your e-mail name (only the part that precedes the @ sign in your e-mail address) into the **POP3 Account** text field. Without this, Explorer will not know which mailbox to look in! The password to enter, in the **Password** field, is the one to open the mailbox on your server. Details of this should have been given to you by your Internet service provider or system administrator when you opened your 'service account'. When you have finished, press **OK** to close the box and save your changes.

The first time the Mail window opens, a message from Microsoft, which has been saved on your hard disc, is displayed, as shown at the top of the next page.

To check your own mail, click the **Send and Receive** Toolbar icon which will download any new messages from your mailbox to your hard disc. You can then read and process your mail at your leisure without necessarily being still connected to the Internet.

With the default set-up, Explorer will only check your mailbox when you click the **Send and Receive** icon.

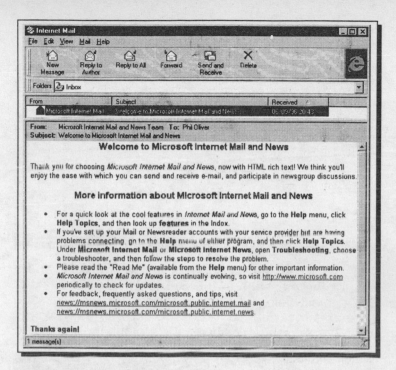

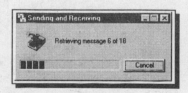

We suggest you make a change in the **Mall**, **Options**, **Read** tab settings sheet. Selecting the **Check for new messages every 10 minutes** option will make the program check your mail box when it starts and at regular intervals while it is open.

A Trial Run

Before explaining in more detail the features of Explorer Mail we will step through the procedure of sending a very simple e-mail message. The best way to test out any unfamiliar e-mail features is to send a test message to your own e-mail address. This saves wasting somebody else's time, and the message can be very quickly checked to see the results.

Click the **New Message** Toolbar icon to open the New Message window, shown below.

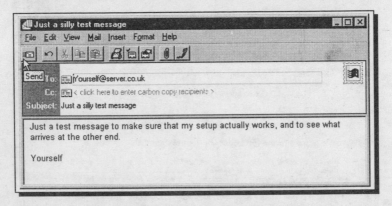

Type your own e-mail address in the **To:** field, and a title for the message in the **Subject:** field. The text in this subject field will form a header for the message when it is received, so it helps to show in a few words what the message is about. Type your message and when you are happy with it, click the **Send** toolbar icon.

The box shown here may then display to explain what has happened to your message. By default, it is stored in an Outbox folder, and

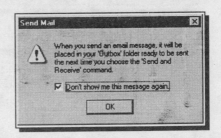

pressing the **Send and Receive** Toolbar icon will send it, hopefully straight into your mailbox. When Explorer next checks for mail, it will find the message and download it into the Inbox folder, as shown on the next page, for you to read and enjoy!

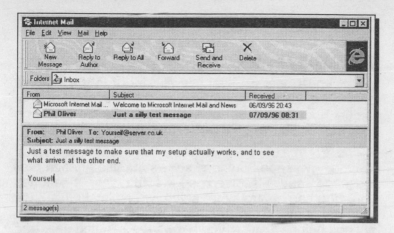

Explorer Mail uses three main windows, the Mail window, which opens first; the Read Message window for reading your mail; and the Send Message window, to compose your outgoing mail messages.

The Mail Window

The Mail window consists of a Toolbar and three panes with the default display shown in our example above. You can choose different pane layouts with the **View**, **Preview Pane** menu command, and you can drag the Toolbar display as in the main Explorer window. We will let you try these for yourself.

The Folders Pane:

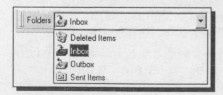

The mail folders pane contains an alphabetical list of your Mail Folders. There are always at least four of these, as shown, but you can add your own folders with the **File**, **Folder**, **Create** menu command from the Mail window. As long as your added folders

85

are empty, you can delete them again with the **File**, **Folder**, **Delete** command.

The Header Pane:

When you select a folder, by clicking it in the Folders pane, the Header pane shows the contents of that folder. Brief details of each message are displayed on one line, as shown on the previous page.

The 'From' column shows the name of the sender of the mail message; 'Subject' shows the title of each mail message, and 'Received' shows the date it reached you. You can control what columns display in this pane with the **View**, **Columns** menu command. The other options being, 'Sent' which shows the sending date and time of the message, 'Size' which gives its file size, and 'To', which shows who it was addressed to.

To sort a list of messages in the Header Pane, you can click the mouse pointer in the title of the column you want the list sorted on.

If you want to keep a message when you have read it, you can use either the **Move to**, or **Copy to** commands from the **Mail** menu to store it in one of the folders in the Folder pane.

The Preview Pane:

When you select a message in the Header pane, by clicking it once, it is displayed in the Preview pane, which takes up the rest of the window. This lets you read the first few lines to see if the message is worth bothering with. If so, double clicking the header, in the Header pane, will open the message in the Read Message window, as shown later in the chapter.

You could use the Preview pane to read all your mail, especially if your messages are all on the short side, but it is easier to process them from the Read Message window.

The Mail Window Toolbar:

 Opens the Send Message window for creating a new mail message, with the To: field blank.

 Opens the Send Message window for replying to the current mail message, with the To: field pre-addressed to the original sender.

 Opens the Send Message window for replying to the current mail message, with the To: field pre-addressed to all that received copies of the original message.

 Opens the Send Message window for forwarding the current mail message. The To: field is blank. The original Subject field is prefixed with Fw:.

 Connects to the mailbox server and downloads waiting messages, which it places in the Inbox folder. Sends any messages waiting in the Outbox folder.

 Deletes the currently selected message and places it in the Deleted Items folder.

The Read Message Window

If you double-click a message in the Header pane of the Mail window the Read Message window is opened, as shown below.

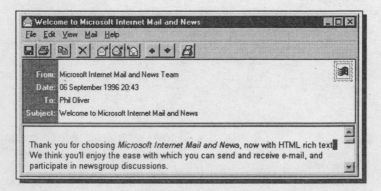

This is the best window to read your mail in. It has its own menu system and Toolbar, which lets you rapidly process and move between the messages in a folder.

The Read Message Toolbar:

Opens the Save Message As box for you to save the message to a disc file. The possible disc formats being, .txt for an ASCII text file, or .eml for a Mail file.

Sends the message to the current Windows printer and uses all the default print settings.

Copies selected text to the Windows clipboard.

Deletes the current message, places it in the Deleted Items folder, and closes the Read Message window.

Opens the Send Message window for replying to the current mail message, with the To: field pre-addressed to the original sender.

Opens the Send Message window for replying to the current mail message, with the To: field pre-addressed to all that received message copies.

Opens the Send Message window for forwarding the current mail message. The To: field is blank. The original Subject field is prefixed with Fw:.

Displays the previous mail message in the Read Message window. The button appears depressed if there are no previous messages.

Displays the next mail message in the Read Message window. The button appears depressed if there are no more messages.

Opens the Address Book window for you to add the details of the message sender.

Viewing File Attachments

Until fairly recently, e-mail on the Internet was good only for short text notes. You couldn't send attachments like formatted document or graphic files with your messages. That has now changed with the advent of MIME, which stands for Multipurpose Internet Mail Extension. With the Internet Explorer you can send Web pages, other formatted documents, photos, sound and video files as attachments to your main e-mail message.

One thing to be careful of though, is to make sure that the person you are sending attachments to has e-mail software capable of decoding them.

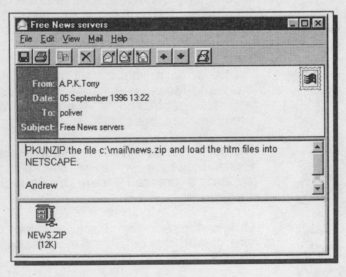

The file attachment appears at the bottom of the message in the Read Message window. To view, or run the file, double-click its icon.

To save a file attachment, use the **File**, **Save Attachments** menu command.

To display, or run, an attachment from the preview pane, click the paper clip file attachment icon in the preview pane header, and then click the file name. To save it from the preview pane, hold down the <Ctrl> key when you click the displayed file name.

The Send Message Window

We briefly looked into the Send Message window earlier in the chapter. This is the window, shown below, that you will use to create any messages you want to send electronically from Explorer, whether from the Mail or the News sections. It is very important to understand its features, so that you can get the most out of it.

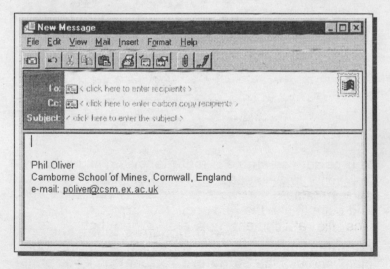

As we saw, this window can be opened by using the **New Message** Toolbar icon, as well as the **Mail, New Message** menu command, or the <Ctrl+N> keyboard shortcut from the main Mail window.

91

It has its own menu system and Toolbar, which let you rapidly prepare and send your new e-mail messages.

Your Own Signature :

If you have created a signature in the **Mail**, **Options**, **Signature** box, as shown below, its text is placed at the end of the message creation area.

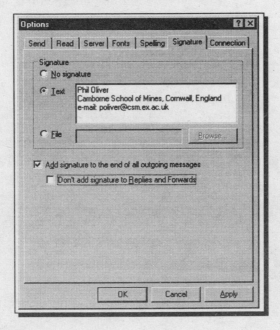

You could also create a more fancy signature file in a text editor like Notepad, or WordPad, including the text and characters you want added to all your messages, and point to it in the **File** section of this box.

We have chosen to **Add signature to the end of all outgoing messages**, but you could leave this option blank and use the **Signature** Toolbar icon if you prefer.

The Send Message Toolbar:

 Sends the created message, either to the recipient, or to the Outbox folder, depending on your settings in the **Mail**, **Options**, **Send** box.

 Undoes the last editing action.

 Cuts selected text to the Windows clipboard.

 Copies selected text to the Windows clipboard.

 Pastes the contents of the Windows clipboard into the current message, at the insertion point.

 Opens the Address Book.

 Checks that any names match your entries in the address book, or are in the correct e-mail address format (name@company).

 Opens the Select Recipients window (which is linked to the Address Book) for you to select who should receive the message.

 Opens the Insert Attachment window for you to select a file to be attached to the current message.

Adds your signature to the bottom of the message, as long as you have specified one in the **Mail**, **Options**, **Signature** box.

Message Formatting

Mail provides quite sophisticated formatting options for an e-mail editor from the **Format** menu, as shown below. These only work if you prepare the message in HTML format, as used in Web documents.

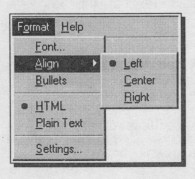

In the **Mail**, **Options**, **Send** box you can set this to be your default mail sending format. To use the format for the current message only, select **HTML** from the **Format** menu, as we have done here.

With HTML, the above Format Toolbar is added to the Send Message window and the top three menu options are then made active. The **Font** command gives you full control of the message font type, and its size and attributes. These functions are also provided by the first six Format Toolbar buttons

The **Align** command, and the three right Toolbar buttons, let you format your message paragraphs with **Left**, **Center** or **Right** alignment.

The **Bullets** menu option, or the Toolbar button shown here, give you an indented bulleted paragraph style suitable for using with lists.

All of these formatting features are quite well demonstrated in Microsoft's opening message to you, which we showed on page 83. You should be able to prepare some very easily readable e-mail messages with these features.

Setting Message Priority

Outgoing e-mail messages can be given one of three

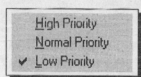

priority ratings, so that their recipients can rank their mail in order of importance. This is only of any real use, though, if the person receiving the message can use the facility.

To set message priorities, either use the **Mail**, **Set Priority** command, or right-click the postage stamp-like icon in the Send Message window. Both open the three choice menu, shown above, the options of which change the stamp icon on the message to one of the following.

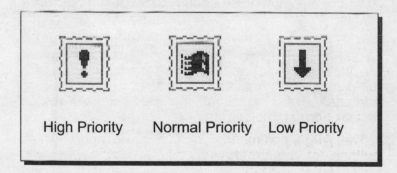

High Priority   Normal Priority   Low Priority

Adding Attachments

If you want to send a Web page, or other type of file as an attachment to your main e-mail message you simply click the **Insert Attachment** Toolbar button and select the file to attach.

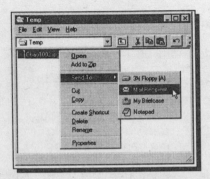

There is an easy way of doing this with Windows 95. You may have noticed that when Internet Mail was installed on your system the new option **Mail Recipient** was placed on your **Send To** menu.

To try this out, open a My Computer window and right-click on a file (any file, it doesn't matter which one). You may have more, or less, options than shown in our example above (depending on your system set-up), but you should have Mail Recipient. Clicking this opens a Send Message window with the attachment file added to the bottom, as shown below.

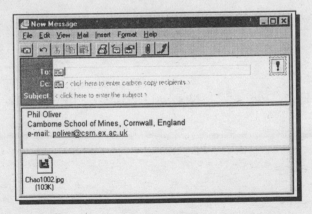

Sending an E-mail

 When you have filled in the address fields typed and formatted the body of your message, added any attachments, and maybe placed a signature, you simply click the **Send** Toolbar button, shown here, to start the transmission process. What happens to the message next depends on your Option settings.

If you want to keep the message and send it later, maybe with several others to save on your telephone bill, make sure the **Send messages immediately** option is not selected in the **Mail**, **Options**, **Send** settings box. In this case, clicking the above **Send** Toolbar icon places the message in the Outbox folder.

When you are ready to send your held messages you click the **Send and Receive** Toolbar icon on the main Mail window. If you forget to do this, Explorer will prompt you with a message box when you attempt to exit the program.

When the **Send messages immediately** option is selected, your messages will be sent on their way as soon as you click the **Send** Toolbar button. This option is best used if you have a permanent connection to the Internet, or your e-mail is being sent over an internal network, or Intranet.

Replying to a Message

When you receive an e-mail message that you want to reply to, Explorer Mail makes it very easy to do. The reply address and the new message subject fields are both added automatically for you. Also, by default, the original message is quoted in the reply window for you to edit as required.

With the message you want to reply to open in the Mail window, either click the **Reply to Author** Toolbar button, use the **Mail**, **Reply to Author** menu command, or use the <Ctrl+R> keyboard shortcut. All open the Send Message window.

Using Quoted Text:

It is almost an e-mail standard now to place the '>' character at the beginning of every line of quoted text in a message. Explorer does this automatically for you.

You should not, however, leave all of the original message in your reply. This is very bad practice, which rapidly makes new messages very large and time consuming to download. You should edit the quoted text, so that it is obvious what you are referring to. Usually one or two lines is enough.

Removing Deleted Messages

Whenever you delete a message it is actually moved to the Deleted Items folder. If ignored, this folder gets

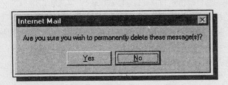

bigger and bigger over time, so you need to either check it every few days and manually re-delete messages you are sure you will

not need again. In which case you are given this last warning message. Or, if you are confident that you will not need this safety net, you can opt to **Empty messages from the 'Deleted Items' folder on exit** in the **Mail**, **Options**, **Read** settings box. You will then have a short time to change your mind before they are finally deleted.

The Address Book

E-mail addresses are often quite complicated and not easy to remember at all. With the Explorer there is a very useful Address Book built in and an almost empty example of one is shown here.

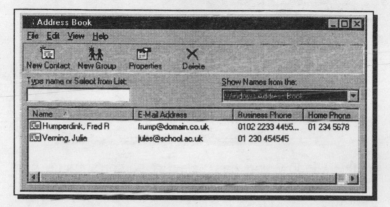

It can be opened from the main Explorer window with the **File**, **Address Book** menu command, or from the Read and Send Message windows by clicking the **Address Book** Toolbar icon.

You can manually add a person's full details and e-mail address, in the Properties box that opens when you click the **New Contact** Toolbar icon. The **New Group** icon lets you create a grouping of e-mail addresses, you can then send mail to everyone in the group with one operation.

We will leave it to you to find your way round this very comprehensive facility. Don't forget that it has its own Help system that you can use.

To send a new message to anyone listed in your Address Book, open a Send Message window and click the **Select Recipients** Toolbar icon, which is shown here.

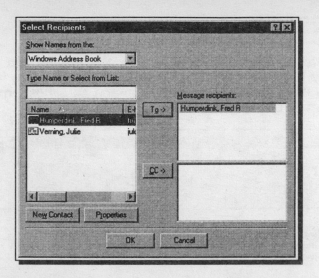

In this window you can select a person's name and click either the **To**-> button to place it in the **To:** field of your message, or the **CC**-> button to place it in the **Cc:** field.

The **New Contact** button lets you add details for a new person to the Address Book, and the **Properties** button lets you edit an existing entry.

The Inbox Assistant

If you are ever in the situation of receiving e-mail messages from a source you do not want to hear from, you can use the Inbox Assistant to filter your incoming messages. Unwanted ones can be placed in your Deleted Items folder straight away. It is also useful for sorting incoming messages and automatically routing them to their correct folders.

To open the Assistant, which is shown on the facing page, use the **Mail**, **Inbox Assistant** menu command. Click the **Add** button and type the criteria you want the incoming message to match in the Properties box.

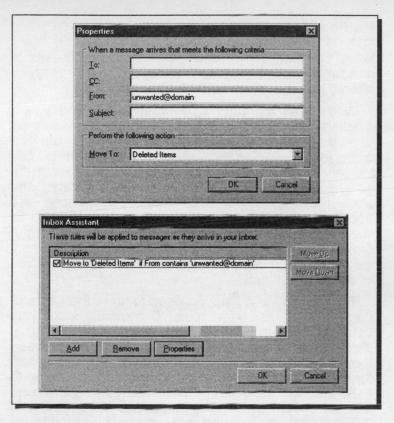

In our example above, we have set the Assistant to intercept any messages from 'unwanted@domain' and send them for immediate deletion.

You can set multiple rules for incoming messages and control the priority that messages are sorted in the list. The higher up a multiple list a condition is the higher will be its priority. Use the **Move Up** and **Move Down** buttons to change priorities.

If an incoming message matches more than one rule, then it is sorted according to the first rule it matches in your list.

Mailing Lists

When you start using e-mail you want to receive lots of messages, but until your friends get active there is often a lull. This is the time to join a mailing list.

Mailing lists are automatic mailing systems where a message sent to a list address is automatically sent on to all the other members of the list. The programs that manage this automatic mailing have names like Listserv, or Majordomo, which usually form part of the List address. Some of these lists are moderated and work much like journals, where submissions are accepted, sometimes edited, and then forwarded to subscribers. Others, however, have no constraints put on their contents! Although the quality and quantity vary from list to list, you can often find a wealth of free information in them.

To subscribe to a list, you need to know the name of the list and its addresses. Commands can vary between different lists, but they often follow the format given below. Note that there is a difference between the address to which you send postings, or messages, for the list, and the address you use for subscribing to it. Be sure to distinguish between these two addresses. One of the most common mistakes made by new Internet users is to send subscription requests to list addresses, which are then forwarded to all the members on the list. Please don't make this mistake, it can be annoying and time consuming for other list readers.

List Subscription commands:

All of these commands go to the subscription address:

sub *listname First Last*	To subscribe to *listname*, with your *First* and *Last* names given.
signoff *listname*	To unsubscribe from a list.

set *listname* nomail To turn off mail from a list if you are going away.

set *listname* mail To turn the mail back on when you return.

Finding a Suitable List:

There are literally thousands of Mailing lists which you can join, covering almost every subject imaginable, from science, to art, to hobbies, and even ones on kinky sex. One of the biggest problems is finding the ones which interest you.

Fortunately, there are several Web sites which give details of Mailing lists. A good one we have used, which includes a search facility and many useful links should be found at

http://www.yahoo.com/Computers_and_Internet

Another one, with lists grouped by topic should be at

http://wwwneosoft.com/internet/paml/bysubj.html

Both of these will put you in direct contact with your selected lists, where you will get instructions on how to subscribe and proceed. Make sure you keep a copy of any instructions, you will need them in the future.

Once you have mastered Mailing lists you need never have an empty mailbox again.

Often Used E-mail Symbols

Once you start receiving messages from lists and other places around the globe, you may encounter some of the following acronyms, and symbols, which people often use to relieve the general boredom of life.

Acronyms:

BTW	By the way
CU	See you (bye)
FAQ	Frequently asked question
FYI	For your information
IMHO	In my humble opinion
IMO	In my opinion
ROTFL	Rolling on the floor laughing
RTFM	Read the manual!
TTYL	Talk to you later

Smileys:

You tilt your head sideways to see them:

:-)	Smiling
:-D	Laughing
;-)	Winking
:-O	Surprise
:-(	Frowning, Sad
:-I	Indifferent
:-/	Perplexed
:-{}	Smiley with a moustache
8-)	Smiley with glasses
<:-|	Dunce
:-X	My lips are sealed
:->	Sarcastic

If these appeal to you, you can get a more comprehensive selection from the *Unofficial Smiley Dictionary* reached at the following Web address:

http://www.eff.org/papers/eegtti/eeg_286.html#SEC287

8. MICROSOFT NEWS

Discussion groups, or 'newsgroups', are a main feature of the Internet and are easily accessed with the Internet Explorer. They are often known as Usenet groups and consist of over 25,000 separate news groups which let you actively take part in discussion on a vast number of topics. In fact almost any subject you could think of is covered, and the number of groups is growing larger all the time.

Explorer News is a program you can use for viewing, and posting (or mailing), messages to these Usenet groups. Unlike e-mail, which is usually 'one-to-one', newsgroups could be said to be 'many-to-many'.

How Usenet Works

Usenet messages are shipped around the world, from host system to host system, using one of several available protocols, that you don't need to bother too much about. Your host server stores all of its Usenet messages in one place, which everybody with an account on the system can access, if they want. That way, no matter how many people actually read a given message, each host has to store only one copy of it. The host systems contact each other regularly and bring themselves up to date with the latest Usenet messages, sometimes this happens thousands of times a day.

Usenet is huge. We have seen it quoted that every day Usenet users transmit over 40 million characters into the system. Some of this information has to be of use! In fact there are so many active groups now, it is unlikely that your server will handle them all. This can be frustrating, if you keep seeing references to a group that you cannot access through your server.

Usenet Newsgroups

The basic building block of Usenet as we have seen is the newsgroup, which is a collection of messages with a related theme. These are arranged in a particular hierarchy that originated in the early 80s. Newsgroup names start with one of a series of broad topic names. For example, newsgroups beginning with **'sci'** should have scientific and engineering content. These broad topics are followed by a series of more specific topic names. **'sci.engr'** groups, for example, are limited to discussion about engineering subjects, and **'sci.engr.mining'** would be a group dedicated to very specific discussion on mining engineering topics.

There are many national and regional groups, including **uk**, but some of the main topic headers are:

alt	Controversial, or unusual topics; not always carried by servers.
bionet	Research biology.
bit.listserv	Conferences originating as Bitnet mailing lists.
biz	Business.
comp	Computers and related subjects.
misc	Discussions that don't fit anywhere else.
news	News about Usenet and its groups.
rec	Hobbies, games and recreation.
sci	Science and engineering, other than research biology.
soc	Social groups, often ethnically related.
talk	Politics and related topics.

With such an almost unlimited choice, you should very soon be able to subscribe to your own unique reading list of newsgroups. Subscribing does not mean you have to pay something, but means that when you enter News you will only see the groups in which you are most interested, and won't have to search through all of the others every time.

Starting Explorer News

The News program is usually opened from the main Explorer window, either with the **Go**, **Read News** menu command, or by clicking the **Mail** Toolbar button and selecting **Read News** from the drop-down menu, as shown here.

Another way is from the Windows 95 **Start** menu, by clicking **Programs**, **Internet Mail**. This way you don't even need to start the Explorer browser.

Internet News Configuration

Before you can access the Usenet groups with Explorer News you must make sure that your details and those of your news server are entered into the Internet News Configuration Wizard.

You will need to enter your name, your e-mail address, the news server you want to connect to, and how you will connect to the server (LAN, manual or by modem). If necessary, you should get the correct entry details from your Internet provider.

In our case we attempted to connect to our server, info.ex.ac.uk, but found that it was not compatible with Explorer News. The command [XOVER] was needed.

This seems to be a common problem with the current version of News. If you get this problem, don't worry, there are hundreds of news servers on the Internet that allow you to connect to them without a password. You should be able to find them with one of the search engines. One we found that worked was 'news2.news.demon.net'. These servers do not always stay permanently available though.

The Newsgroups Window

The initial set-up procedure finishes by downloading a list of all the groups available on the news server. As there are well over 20,000 available to some servers this can take quite a while. When this is done, a window similar to ours below opens and you can see what newsgroups are available to you.

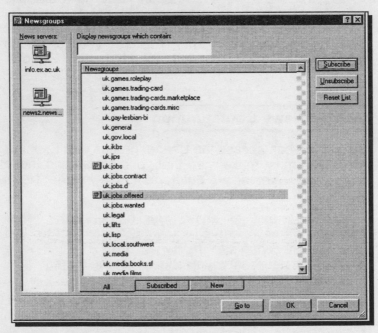

If you are subscribed to more than one server, the **Newsgroups** pane lists the groups available from the server selected in the **News Servers** pane.

If you scroll down through the list of groups, almost at the bottom you should find some that start with **uk**. In our example, we selected **uk.jobs.offered** and clicked the **Go to** button, which is an easy way to have a look at the contents of a group.

A one line header (for each of the 136 messages contained in the group), was loaded into the Message Header pane of the Explorer News window, as shown below. And they say we have high unemployment!

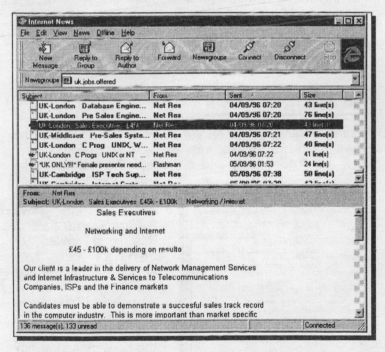

As soon as one of these headers is selected, the message itself appears in the Preview pane below it. This can take a few moments, don't forget it has to be downloaded over the network from your server.

Subscribing to a Group:

If you think a group looks interesting and would be useful in the future, you should subscribe to it. To do this, locate it in the Newsgroups window and click the **Subscribe** button. A newspaper icon is placed alongside the group name in the listing. To remove a group from your subscribed list, you simply select it and click the **Unsubscribe** button.

Once you have selected all the groups you regularly want to keep tabs on, click the **Subscribed** tab button at the bottom of the list.

In the future, each time you open the Newsgroups window, it will only display your chosen list. At any time while this window is open you can click **All** to see a complete listing again, or **New** to see any new groups.

Adding a News Server

To add another news server to your set-up, open the **News**, **Options**, **Server** settings box, as shown below. Click the **Add** button and complete the details in the

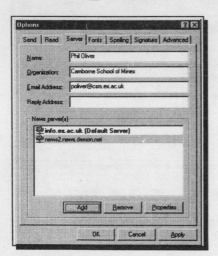

next opened dialogue box. Enter the server name in the **News Server Name** field. If this is a closed, or members only type server, complete the log on details which you should have been given. Otherwise click **OK**. Selecting **Yes** to the next message box will download the server groups. The **OK** button will then complete the process.

The Explorer News Window

The News window, which is shown on page 109, is almost the same as the Mail window, and like the Mail window contains three panes: a Newsgroups pane, a Message Header pane, and a Preview pane.

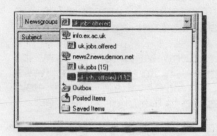

You open the Newsgroups pane by clicking the down arrow on the right hand end. As shown here, this lists the available servers, the subscribed groups in each, and some folders for handling your newsgroup correspondence.

Clicking on a group in the Newsgroups pane, displays a listing of the group's current headers in the Message Header pane, which has four columns:

Subject   Shows the subject line of the message.

From   Gives the 'name' of the sender of the news message.

Sent   States the date and time the message was posted to the group.

Size   Gives the number of lines in the message.

You can sort messages by any of the columns and in ascending or descending order, by clicking in the column header. You can also add, remove, or rearrange the columns, and sort them, with the **View**, **Columns** menu command.

Clicking on a message header, downloads and displays the message body text in the Preview pane.

The News Toolbar

 New Message
Opens a Send Message window for creating a new e-mail message, with the To: field blank.

 Reply to Group
Opens the Send Message window for sending a message to be posted in the currently selected newsgroup.

 Reply to Author
Opens the Send Message window for replying privately to the current news message, with the To: field pre-addressed to the original sender.

 Forward
Opens the Send Message window for forwarding the current news message. The To: field is blank. The original Subject field is prefixed with Fw:.

 Newsgroups
Opens the Newsgroups window in which you select which news server to use and the groups to subscribe to.

 Connect
Attempts to make a connection with the selected news server and to download selected messages or headers.

 Disconnect
Disconnects from the currently connected news server.

 Stop
Stops the current downloading operation. This option is only available when the download Status Indicator (on its right) is rotating.

112

The Read Message Window

Double-clicking on a message header in the News window, opens a Read Message window with the message in it, as shown below.

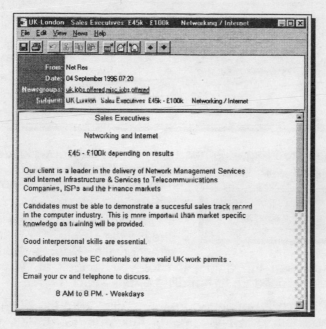

This window has its own menu and Toolbar. Moving the mouse pointer over a Toolbar button shows what the button's action will be.

Postings Containing Pictures

If you have time to explore the many thousands of **alt** groups, you will find that a lot of them contain messages with picture files attached that are (or should be) relevant to the group name. On the next page we show one being downloaded from a group that does not normally need censoring, but be warned, many of them do!

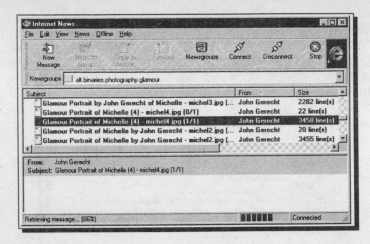

When the image file has been completely downloaded, a paper clip icon is placed on the title bar of the Preview pane, as shown here.

Clicking this icon once will show the name of the attached file. Double-clicking it will open the actual file for you to look at. A very similar procedure to handling e-mail attachments.

To save an attached image to disc from the preview pane, hold down the <Ctrl> key when you click the displayed file name.

To save a file attachment from the Read Message window, use the **File**, **Save Attachments** menu command.

Replying to Messages

As long as you have selected to **Make Microsoft Internet Mail your default e-mail program** in the **Mail**, **Options**, **Send** settings box, the News window Toolbar icons will use the Mail facilities to easily send messages of three different types. The **Reply to Group** icon addresses your message to the current newsgroup for all to read. The **Reply to Author** icon addresses an e-mail message to the individual who posted the current news message. Be very careful not to mix these up, the result could be embarrassing if you post a personal message to the whole group, for maybe millions of people to read!

The **Forward** icon prepares an e-mail with a copy of the current message, for you to address and complete.

If you need to know more, may we suggest you go back a few pages, as all the e-mail facilities discussed in the last chapter are available to you.

Threaded Messages

When a message is placed on a newsgroup, often someone replies and then a 'thread' of discussion is formed about the original message topic.

Explorer News messages are threaded by default, as long as **Auto expand conversation threads** is checked in the **News**, **Options**, **Read** settings sheet, replies being placed with the original messages.

If you want the message list to display only the original message in a thread, select the first message, and then use the **View**, **Collapse** menu command, or click the minus (-) sign next to the original message.

If you then want the list to display all of a thread, select the first message, and then action the **View**, **Expand** menu command, or click the plus (+) sign next to the original message.

The edited News Help window shown on the following page explains clearly how you can recognise the Read and Thread status of any news message in the Message Header pane of a News window.

Identifying Internet News message list icons

The following icons indicate whether a thread is expanded or collapsed, and whether messages and headers are marked as read or unread.

This icon	Indicates
➕	This level of the thread is collapsed. Click this icon to expand the thread.
➖	This level of the thread is expanded. Click this icon to collapse the thread.
🗐	The message has been marked read, and the header and body are cached. The heading appears in light type.
🗋	The message has been marked as read, and the header is cached. The heading appears in light type.
🗐	The message has not been marked as read, and the header and body are cached. The heading appears in bold type.
🗋	The message has not been marked as read, and the header is cached. The heading appears in bold type.

Off-Line Viewing

If, like most of us, you are usually busy and don't have time to wait for long newsgroup messages to be downloaded, you can set up a batch download process and view selected group headers and/or messages off-line later on.

With the **Offline** menu options you can mark individual messages, threads, or entire newsgroups for downloading. To start the process use the **Offline**, **Post and Download** command.

116

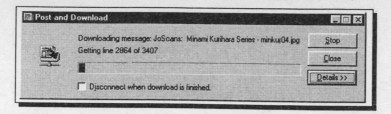

A Post and Download box, similar to the one above, will show you how the download process is going. If you want to know what download jobs are still to be processed, click the **Details** button.

When the download procedure is complete, you can return to the News Window and the icons, shown on the previous page, will then show the status of any saved, or cached, headers or messages.

Newsgroup Caches

Each newsgroup you subsrcibe to has its own cache file on your computer and everything you download from that group, either manually or for off-line viewing, is saved in this cache. When you select to view at item that is stored in a cache it is 'instantly' displayed, as it does not have to be downloaded. This is all very well, but if you are not careful you can fill your hard disc up with material you don't even know you are keeping.

Controlling the Caches :

The **News**, **Options**, **Advanced** settings sheet gives you control of the size of all your cached message files, as we show in the dialogue box at the top of the next page.

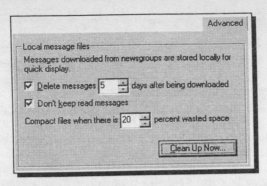

The settings shown above will prevent things getting too much out of hand, but every now and then you should click the **Clean Up Now** button to manually compact, delete, or remove messages from all or specific message files. This clean-up procedure is usually known as 'purging.' The same 'manual clean up' options are also available from the News menu with the **File**, **Clean Up Files** command.

Purging unused, old, or large newsgroups can increase your free hard disc space enormously. Most news servers remove old messages and headers on a regular basis, sometimes even weekly. The next time you connect to a newsgroup you've purged, your cache is rebuilt with just the current messages and headers from the server.

On Your Own

You should, by now, have enough basic knowledge to happily venture forth into the unknown.

Good luck, but please remember that there are millions of other newsgroup readers, and you never know where, or who, they are. Watch what you say in your postings, there is enough rubbish there already.

9. BEHAVIOUR ON THE INTERNET

As we saw in the first chapter, the Internet has grown up without any real control. It has grown, just like Topsy, but some of the behaviour you see there is not always quite as nice. We will not talk about pornography, or worse. If that is what you want, it is probably there to be found (as in most major cities of the world), but increasingly now it is hidden behind closed doors. Most really dubious sites require membership and payment, especially after the recent legal moves in the US Senate and Germany. If you have children that use your computer to surf the Web, the Internet Explorer has a security feature to enable you to control what they are exposed to, this is briefly discussed at the end of the chapter.

Parts of the media seem to have latched onto the idea that anything illegal or unusual that people get up to is because they saw how to do it on the Internet. It seems to have become something of a scapegoat. We have seen this recently regarding the making of bombs and the perpetration of credit card fraud.

The Internet does have its problem children, just like any other area of our society. Maybe one of the problems is just that, children. They seem to run wild in some of the newsgroups, posting all manner of objectionable and misspelled messages.

We will very briefly mention some of the more dubious behaviour patterns you may encounter on your way round the Internet, especially in the newsgroups, and to a lesser extent the mailing lists.

Internet Flames

A flame is a particularly nasty, personal attack on somebody for something he, or she, has written in a posting. Newsgroups are notorious for flaming (burning people up). This can sometimes lead to long and drawn-out discussions on what really are stupid matters. These 'flame wars' can sometimes be fun to watch at first, but quickly grow boring, and become a general waste of everyone's time and mail space.

But, be warned, once you start posting to groups you may well upset someone, without even meaning to. If they are vicious, you may get flamed.

Spam, Spam, Bacon and Spam

Spamming, on the Internet, is the practice of sending a message to a very large number of newsgroups and mailing lists. It is named after the Monty Python sketch, where you could have what you liked in the restaurant as long as it had spam with it. A spammer gives you little choice, you have to download his posting, but you don't have to read it.

It will not be long before you encounter this 'problem' in some form, or other. Often a product, service, or a get rich quick scheme is being offered. We tend to ignore them and hope they will go away.

Other Usenet Freaks

There are a number of other Usenet types you'll soon come to recognise, and love:

Ones that think their topic of interest should be forced on everyone else as frequently as possible. Often posting dozens of messages to unrelated groups, sometimes with ethnic contents.

Ones that take pages of message to get nowhere. This often includes excessive quoting by including the entire message in their reply, rather than deleting the irrelevant portions.

Ones who enjoy insulting others and post nasty, or even obscene, messages in unrelated newsgroups.

Ones who include enormous signatures at the end of their postings, often including enormous text graphics. These are harmless, but can be annoying.

Not really in the same category, but the term 'lurker' is commonly used and needs some explanation. It usually seems to be used derogatively, but we do not know why. The best definition we have found is:

> **lurker:**[1] **/n./** One of the 'silent majority' in an electronic forum; one who posts occasionally or not at all but is known to read the group's postings regularly. This term is not pejorative and indeed is casually used reflexively: "Oh, I'm just lurking."
> Often used in 'the lurkers', the hypothetical audience for the group's {flamage} - emitting regulars. When a lurker speaks up for the first time, this is called 'delurking'.

Most of us, and especially new users, must be classified as lurkers for much of the time.

Some Internet Etiquette

Often called 'netiquette' the following list, we recently found[2], makes good reading and should help you avoid most flames on the Net:

1   DON'T include the entire contents of a previous posting in your reply.

    DO cut mercilessly. Leave just enough to indicate what you're responding to. NEVER include mail headers except maybe the 'From:' line. If you can't figure out how to delete lines in

---

[1]   The on-line hacker Jargon File, version 3.3.3, 25 MAR 1996
[2]   Patrick Crispen's Internet Roadmap, 1994

your mailer software, paraphrase or re-type the quoted material.

2 DON'T reply to a point in a posting without quoting or paraphrasing what you're responding to and who said it. Reason: a dozen postings may occur between the original message and your reply.

DO quote (briefly) or paraphrase. If the original 'Subject:' line was 'Big dogs' make sure yours says 'Re: Big dogs'. Some REPLY functions do this automatically. By net convention, included lines are preceded by '>' (greater-than signs). Some mail editors and newsreaders do this automatically. Others require you to do it manually or set the 'indent character' to '>'.

At some sites your reply may get there before the original.

3 DON'T send a message saying "Why doesn't anybody say anything about X?"

It's always a risk to start a new topic (often called a thread). The group may have just finished a long, bitter war about that very subject. But if you want to take the risk, SAY SOMETHING yourself about the subject.

4 DON'T send lines longer than 70 characters. This is a kindness to folks with terminal-based mail editors or newsreaders. Some mail gateways truncate extra characters turning your deathless prose into gibberish.

Some mail editor tools only SEEM to insert line breaks for you, but actually don't, so that every paragraph is one immense line. Learn what your mail editor does.

5 DON'T SEND A MESSAGE IN ALL CAPS. CAPITALISED MESSAGES ARE HARDER TO READ THAN LOWER CASE OR MIXED CASE.

DO use normal capitalisation. Separate your paragraphs with blank lines. Make your message inviting to your potential readers.

6 DON'T betray confidences. It is all too easy to quote a personal letter in a posting to the entire group.

DO read the 'To:' and 'Cc:' lines in your message before you send it. Are you SURE you want the mail to go there?

7 DON'T make statements which can be interpreted as official positions of your organisation or offers to do business. Saying "Boy, I'd sure like to have one of them Crays" could result in a truck at your loading dock and a bill in the mail even larger than a student loan.

DO treat every post as though you were sending a copy to your boss, your minister, and your worst enemy.

8 DON'T rely on the ability of your readers to tell the difference between serious statements and satire, or sarcasm. It's hard to write funny. It's even harder to write satire.

DO remember that no one can hear your tone of voice. Use smileys, like:

:-) or **;^)**

turn your head anti-clockwise to see the smile.

You can also use capitals for emphasis, or use Net conventions for italics and underlines as in:

"You said the guitar solo on "Comfortably Numb" from Pink Floyd's, The Wall, was *lame*? Are you OUT OF YOUR MIND???!!!"

9 DON'T make a posting that says nothing but "Me, too." This is most annoying when combined with (1) or (2) above. Another one is "I don't know."

DO remember the immortal words of Martin Farquhar Tupper (1810-1889): *"Well-timed silence hath more eloquence than speech."*

Censoring Your Web Browser

The Internet Explorer allows you to control what Web sites your children can access. This is located on the **View**, **Options**, **Security** settings sheet shown here.

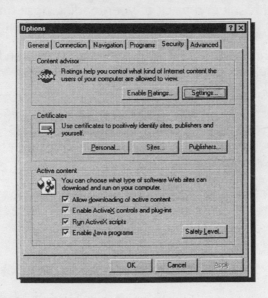

Clicking the **Enable Ratings** button will ask you to establish a password. You have to do this before you can go any further, but please don't forget it or you will find yourself re-installing the Explorer in the future!

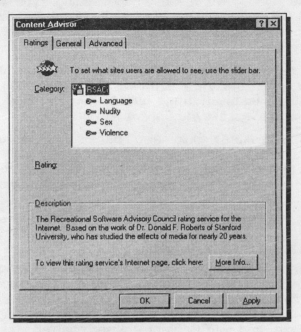

The Content Adviser control window is then opened, as shown above, which has four sliders to allow you to set the degree of language, nudity, sex and violence you want your children (or other users) to be exposed to.

This facility depends on Web sites having a rating system 'attached to them'. The Content Adviser then filters out unsuitable sites and prohibits access to them. The default site rating service is provided by the Recreational Software Advisory Council. There is the facility to select others in the **Advanced** tab section.

By default, if a Web site does not have a rating your users will not be able to access it. They will be presented with a blacked out screen if they try. You can alter this, however, in the **General** tab section, by checking the **Users can see sites which have no rating** option. Also in this section you can use the **Change Password** feature.

When you have made all the settings you want, press **OK** enough times to close the Content Adviser. You have now censored your computer, probably for the first time!

To cancel, or change, your security settings in the future, open the **View**, **Options**, **Security** sheet and click the **Disable Ratings** button. You will need your password to access the Content Adviser.

This measure could also be usefully used by organisations to limit their personnel to specific sites on the Internet. This would not be a popular measure, but would almost certainly reduce the amount of wasted time.

A Feature for the Future:

We feel this feature is a commendable attempt by Microsoft to make surfing the Web a safer place for your children, but it does depend on all the 'non-exotic' sites getting rated. At the moment this is anything but the case, and with Content Adviser enabled you may as well turn off your computer.

10. GLOSSARY OF TERMS

Agent

A search tool that automatically seeks out relevant on-line information.

Anonymous ftp

Anonymous ftp allows you to connect to a remote computer and transfer public files back to your local computer without the need to have a user ID and password.

Application

Software (program) designed to carry out certain activity, such as word processing.

Archie

Archie is an Internet service that allows you to locate files that can be downloaded via FTP.

Association

An identification of a filename extension to a program. This lets Windows open the program when its files are selected.

ASCII

A binary code representation of a character set. The name stands for 'American Standard Code for Information Interchange'.

Attributes

Indicate whether a file is read-only, hidden or system and if it has changed since it was last backed up.

Backup

To make a back-up copy of a file or a disc for safekeeping.

Bandwidth

The range of transmission frequencies a network can use. The greater the bandwidth the more information that can be transferred over a network.

Base memory	The first 1 MB of random access memory.
Batch file	An ASCII formatted file that contains DOS commands which can be executed by the computer.
Baud	The unit of measurement used to describe data transmission speed. One baud is one bit per second.
BBS	Bulletin Board System, a computer equipped with software and telecoms links that allow it to act as an information host for remote computer systems.
BinHex	A file conversion format that converts binary files to ASCII text files.
BIOS	The Basic Input/Output System. It allows the core of a PC's operating system to communicate with the hardware.
Bit	A binary digit; the smallest unit of information that can be stored, either as a 1 or as a 0.
Bitmap	A technique for managing the image displayed on a computer screen.
Browse	A button in some Windows dialogue boxes that lets you view a list of files and folders before you make a selection.
Browser	A program, like the Internet Explorer, that lets you graphically view World Wide Web pages.
Buffer	RAM memory allocated to store data being read from disc.

Byte	A grouping of binary digits (0 or 1) which represent information.
Cache	An area of memory, or disc space, reserved for data, which speeds up down-loading.
Card	A removable printed-circuit board that is plugged into a computer expansion slot.
CD-ROM	Compact Disc - Read Only Memory; an optical disc from which information may be read but not written.
Check box	A small box in a dialogue box that can be selected (X), or cleared (empty).
Click	To quickly press and release a mouse button.
Client	A computer that has access to services over a computer network. The computer providing the services is a server.
Client application	A windows application that can accept linked, or embedded, objects.
Clipboard	A temporary storage area of memory, where text and graphics are stored with the Windows cut and copy actions.
Close	To remove a dialogue box or window, or to exit a program.
Code page	A table in Windows that defines which extended ASCII character set is used in a document.
Command	An instruction given to a computer to carry out a particular action.

Command line	The line in an MS-DOS window, or screen, into which you enter DOS commands.
Command Prompt	The prompt (e.g. C>) which appears on the command line to let you know that DOS is ready to receive a command.
Computer name	The name that identifies a specific computer to other users of a network.
Configuration	A general purpose term referring to the way you have your computer set up.
CONFIG.SYS	A special file that allows the system to be configured closer to requirement.
CPU	The Central Processing Unit; the main chip that executes all instructions entered into a computer.
Cyberspace	Originated by William Gibson in his novel 'Neuromancer', now used to describe the Internet and the other computer networks.
DDE	Dynamic data exchange - a process that enables you to exchange data between two or more Windows programs.
Dial-up Connection	A popular form of Net connection for the home user, over standard telephone lines.
Direct Connection	A permanent connection between your computer system and the Internet. Often referred to as a leased-line connection.

Default	The command, device or option automatically chosen.
Desktop	The Windows screen working background, on which you place icons, folders, etc.
Device driver	A special file that must be loaded into memory for Windows to be able to address a specific procedure or hardware device.
Device name	A logical name used by DOS to identify a device, such as LPT1 or COM1 for the parallel or serial printer.
Dialogue box	A window displayed on the screen to allow the user to enter information.
Dimmed	Unavailable menu options shown in a different colour.
Directory	An area on disc where information relating to a group of files is kept. Known as a folder in Windows 95.
Disc	A device on which you can store programs and data.
Disc file	A collection of program code, or data, that is stored under a given name on a disc.
Disconnect	To detach a drive, port or computer from a shared device, or to break an Internet connection.
Document	When used in reference to the Web, a document is any file containing text, media or hyperlinks that can be transferred from an HTTP server to a browser.

	Otherwise it is a file produced by an application program.
Domain	A group of devices, servers and computers on a network.
DOS	Disc Operating System. A collection of small specialised programs that allow interaction between user and computer.
DOS prompt	The prompt displayed in an MS-DOS window, or screen, such as A> or C>, indicating that DOS is ready to accept commands.
Double-click	To quickly press and release a mouse button twice.
Download	To transfer to your computer a file, or data, from another computer.
DPI	Dots Per Inch - a resolution standard for laser printers.
Drag	To move an object on the screen by pressing and holding down the left mouse button while moving the mouse.
Drive name	The letter followed by a colon which identifies a floppy or hard disc drive.
EISA	Extended Industry Standard Architecture, for construction of PCs with the Intel 32 bit micro-processor.
Embedded object	Information in a document that is 'copied' from its source application. Selecting the object opens the creating application from within the document.

Enter key	The key that is pressed after entering data on the command line.
Expanded memory	This is memory outside the conventional RAM (first 640 KB) and is used by some MS-DOS software to store data and run applications.
Extended memory	This is memory above the 1-MB memory address, all of which is used by Windows 95.
FAQ	Acronym for Frequently Asked Questions. A common feature on the Internet, FAQs are files of answers to commonly asked questions.
FAT	The File Allocation Table. An area on disc where information is kept on which part of the disc a file is located.
File extension	The optional suffix following the period in a filename. Windows uses this to identify the source application program.
Filename	The name given to a file. In Windows 95 this can be up to 256 characters long.
Filespec	File specification made up of drive, path and filename.
Firewall	Security measures designed to protect a networked system from unauthorised access.
Fixed disc	The hard disc of a computer.

Floppy disc	A removable disc on which information can be stored magnetically.
Folder	An area used to store a group of files, usually with a common link.
Font	A graphic design representing a set of characters, numbers and symbols.
Formatting	The process of preparing a disc so that it can store information, or of controlling the visual layout of a document.
FTP	File Transfer Protocol. The procedure for connecting to a remote computer and transferring files back to your local computer.
Function key	One of the series of 10 or 12 keys marked with the letter F and a numeral, used for specific operations.
Gopher	A text oriented, hierarchically organised, tool used to locate online resources.
Graphics card	A device that controls the display on the monitor and other allied functions.
GUI	A Graphic User Interface, such as Windows 95, the software front-end meant to provide an attractive and easy to use interface.
Hardcopy	Output on paper.
Hard disc	A device built into the computer for holding programs and data.

Hardware	The equipment that makes up a computer system, excluding the programs or software.
Help	A Windows system that gives you instructions and additional information on using a program.
Highlight	The change to a reverse-video appearance when a menu item or area of text is selected.
HMA	High Memory Area; the first 64 KB of memory beyond the end of the base memory.
Home Page	The document displayed when you first open your Web browser, or the first document you come to at a Web site.
Hotlist	A list of frequently used Web locations and URL addresses.
Host	A computer acting as an information or communications server.
HTML	HyperText Markup Language, the format used in documents on the World Wide Web.
HTTP	HyperText Transport Protocol the system used to link and transfer hypertext documents on the Web.
Hypermedia	Hypertext extended to include linked multi-media.
Hypertext	A system that allows documents to be cross-linked so that the reader can explore related links, or documents, by clicking on a highlighted word or symbol.

Icon	A small graphic image that represents a function or object. Clicking on an icon produces an action.
Insertion point	A flashing bar that shows where typed text will be entered into a document.
Interface	A device that allows you to connect a computer to its peripherals.
Internet	The global system of computer networks.
IRQ	Interrupt request lines - hardware lines used by devices to signal the processor that they are ready to send, or receive, data.
ISA	Industry Standard Architecture; a standard for internal connections in PCs.
ISDN	Integrated Services Digital Network, a telecom standard using digital transmission technology to support voice, video and data communications applications over regular telephone lines.
Key combination	When two or more keys are pressed simultaneously, such as <Ctrl+Esc>.
Kilobyte	(KB); 1024 bytes of information or storage space.
LAN	Local Area Network; PCs, workstations or minis sharing files and peripherals within the same site.

LCD	Liquid Crystal Display.
Linked object	A placeholder for an object inserted into a destination document.
Links	The hypertext connections between Web pages.
Local	A resource that is located on your computer, not linked to it over a network.
Log on	To gain access to a network.
Long filename	In Windows 95 the name given to a file can be up to 256 characters long.
MCA	Micro Channel Architecture; IBM's standard for construction of PCs introduced in the 1990s.
MCI	Media Control Interface - a standard for files and multi-media devices.
Megabyte	(MB); 1024 kilobytes of information or storage space.
Megahertz	(MHz); Speed of processor in millions of cycles per second.
Memory	Part of computer consisting of storage elements organised into addressable locations that can hold data and instructions.
Menu	A list of available options in an application.
Menu bar	The horizontal bar that lists the names of menus.
Microprocessor	The calculating chip within a computer.

MIDI	Musical Instrument Digital Interface - enables devices to transmit and receive sound and music messages.
MIME	Multipurpose Internet Mail Extensions, a messaging standard that allows Internet users to exchange e-mail messages enhanced with graphics, video and voice.
MIPS	Million Instructions Per Second; measures speed of a system.
Monitor	The display device connected to your PC, also called a screen.
Mouse	A device used to manipulate a pointer around your display and activate processes by pressing buttons.
MS-DOS	Microsoft's implementation of the Disc Operating System for PCs.
Multimedia	The use of photographs, music and sound and movie images in a presentation.
Multi-tasking	Performing more than one operation at the same time.
NCSA	National Center for Supercomputing Applications. A US federal funded organisation for the research and development of high-technology resources for the scientific community.
Network	A computer network is an interconnection of computers allowing the exchange and sharing of resources (files, data, computing power).

Network server	Central computer which stores files for several linked computers.
NNTP	Network News Transfer Protocol A common method of article transfer over Usenet.
Node	A device attached to a network, which uses the network as a means of communication and has an address on the network.
Operating System	A group of programs that translates your commands to the computer.
Page	A Web page, as used in a browser, is the entire document, however long.
Password	A unique character string used to gain access to a network, program, or mailbox.
PATH	The location of a file in the directory tree.
Peripheral	Any device attached to a PC.
PIF file	Program information file - gives information to Windows about an MS-DOS application.
Pixel	A picture element on screen; the smallest element that can be independently assigned colour and intensity.
POP	Point of Presence, the location of an Internet service provider, where users dial to connect to the host computer.
Port	An input/output address through which your PC interacts with external devices.

PPP	Point-to-Point Protocol, a connection where phone lines and a modem can be used to connect to the Internet.
Print queue	A list of print jobs waiting to be sent to a printer.
Program	A set of instructions which cause a computer to perform tasks.
Prompt	The MS-DOS prompt displayed on the command line, such as A> or C>, indicating that DOS is ready to accept commands.
Protected mode	The operating mode of 386 (and higher) processors, which allows more than 1 MB of memory to be addressed.
Protocol	A set of standards that define how traffic and communications are handled by a computer or network routers. The specific protocol used on the Internet is TCP/IP.
PS/2	The range of PCs first introduced by IBM in late 1980s.
RAM	Random Access Memory. The computer's volatile memory. Data held in it is lost when power is switched off.
Real mode	MS-DOS mode, typically used to run programs, such as MS-DOS games, that will not run under Windows.
Resource	A directory, or printer, that can be shared over a network.
Right-click	To click and release the right mouse button, which often opens

	a context sensitive menu in a Windows application.
ROM	Read Only Memory. A PC's non-volatile memory. Data is written into this memory at manufacture and is not affected by power loss.
Root directory	The main disc directory under which a number of sub-directories can be created.
Router	A communications device used to transmit over a network via the most efficient route possible.
Screen saver	A display program that moves images on an inactive screen.
Scroll bar	A bar that appears at the right side or bottom edge of a window.
Search Engine	A program that helps users find information across the Internet.
Sector	Disc space, normally 512 bytes long.
Serial interface	An interface that transfers data as individual bits; each operation has to be completed before the next starts.
Server	A computer system that manages and delivers information for client computers.
Shared resource	Any device, program or file that is available to network users.
Shareware	Software that is available on public networks and bulletin boards. Users are expected to pay a nominal amount to the software developer.

Site	A server, or a collection of linked Web pages at a single location.
Software	The programs and instructions that control your PC.
SLIP	Serial Line Internet Protocol, a method of Internet connection that enables computers to use phone lines and a modem to connect to the Internet without having to connect to a host.
Socket	An end-point for sending and receiving data between computers.
Spooler	Software which handles transfer of information to a store where it will be used by a peripheral device.
SSL	Secure Sockets Layer, the standard transmission security protocol developed by Netscape, which has been put into the public domain.
SVGA	Super Video Graphics Array; it has all the VGA modes but with 256, or more, colours.
Swap file	An area of your hard disc used to store temporary operating files, also known as virtual memory.
System disc	A disc containing files to enable MS-DOS to start up.
Tags	Formatting codes used in HTML documents, which indicate how parts of a document will appear when displayed.

TCP/IP	Transmission Control Protocol/ Internet Protocol, combined protocols that perform the transfer of data between two computers. TCP monitors and ensures the correct transfer of data. IP receives the data, breaks it up into packets, and sends it to a network within the Internet.
Telnet	A program which allows users to remotely use computers across networks.
Text file	An unformatted file of text characters saved in ASCII format.
Toolbar	A bar containing icons giving quick access to commands.
Toggle	To turn an action on and off with the same switch.
TrueType fonts	Fonts that can be scaled to any size and print as they show on the screen.
UMB	A block of upper memory made available by a 386 memory manager into which memory resident software can be loaded.
Upper memory	The 384 KB of memory between the top of conventional memory and the end of the base memory.
URL	Uniform Resource Locator, the addressing system used on the Web, containing information about the method of access, the server to be accessed and the path of the file to be accessed.
User ID	A one word name used to identify a specific user of a specific

	computer or network. Usually assigned by the system administrator and often includes a portion of the individual's name.
Usenet	The global news-reading network.
Veronica	A search utility that helps find information on Gopher servers.
Virtual machine	A logical computer that Windows 95 creates in memory.
Virtual memory	See swap file.
Volume label	An identifying label written to a disc when it is first formatted.
WAIS	Wide Area Information Service, a Net-wide system for looking up specific information in Internet databases.
Web	See World Wide Web.
Web Page	An HTML document that is accessible on the Web.
Wildcard character	A character that can be included in a filename to indicate any other character (?), or group of characters (*).
World Wide Web	A network of hypertext based multimedia information servers. Web browsers, such as the Internet Explorer, can be used to view any information on the Web.
Zine	An electronic magazine accessed through the Web.

APPENDIX A
KEYBOARD SHORTCUTS

The following keyboard actions are the standard shortcuts for working with the Internet Explorer programs.

Web Browser Shortcuts:

Shortcut	Action
Shortcut	*Action*

General

F5	Refresh the current page
Esc	Stop downloading a page
Ctrl+O	Go to a new location
Ctrl+N	Open a new browser window
Ctrl+S	Save the current page
Ctrl+P	Print the current page or frame
Enter	Activate a selected hyperlink

Viewing documents

Sh+BkSp	Go to next page
BkSp	Go to previous page
Sh+F10	Display object menu for a hyperlink
Sh+Ctrl+Tab	Move between frames
↑	Scroll up a document
↓	Scroll down a document
PgUp	Large scroll up a document
PgDn	Large scroll down a document
Home	Move to the beginning of a document
End	Move to the end of a document

Keyboard shortcuts for Internet Mail:

Shortcut	*Action*
General	
F1	Open help topics
Ctrl+A	Select All

Main Mail Window

Ctrl+O	Open the selected message
Ctrl+Space	Mark a message as read
Tab	Move between window panes

Main and Read Message Windows

Ctrl+D	Delete a message
Ctrl+F	Forward a message
Ctrl+I	Go to your Inbox
Ctrl+M	Send and receive mail
Ctrl+N	Open a new message
Ctrl+P	Print the selected message
Ctrl+R	Reply to the author
Sh+Ctrl+R	Reply to all
Ctrl+>	Go to next message in the list
Ctrl+<	Go to previous message in the list
Alt+Enter	View properties of selected message

Send Message Window

F3	Find text
Esc	Close a message
Ctrl+K	Check names
Ctrl+Enter	Send a message

Keyboard shortcuts for Internet News:

Shortcut	*Action*

General

F1	Open help topics
Ctrl+A	Select All

Main News Window

Sh+Ctrl+A	Mark all as read
Ctrl+O	Open the selected message
Ctrl+W	Go to a newsgroup
Ctrl+Space	Mark a message as read
Tab	Move between window panes
← or +	Expand a thread
→ or -	Collapse a thread
Space	Fill the preview pane with the body of the selected message

Main and Read Message Windows

F5	Refresh headers and articles
Ctrl+F	Forward a message
Ctrl+G	Post a reply to the newsgroup
Ctrl+N	Post new message to the newsgroup
Ctrl+P	Print the selected message
Ctrl+R	Reply to the author
Ctrl+>	Go to the next message in the list
Ctrl+<	Go to previous message in the list
Alt+Enter	View properties of selected message

Send Message Window

Sh+Ctrl+F	Find text
Esc	Close a message
Ctrl+K	Check names
Alt+S	Send a message
F7	Check spelling

APPENDIX B
INTERNET FILE FORMATS

All of the file formats found on the Internet can be broken into one of two types: **ASCII** text files you can view with WordPad or Notepad, and **Binary** which contain non-ASCII characters and cannot be viewed.

We include here a guide to the most common Internet file formats with details of how some of them can be viewed, or played.

Plain Text (ASCII) Files:

.html/.htm   The language in which Web documents are authored. File type is ASCII and requires a Web browser like Explorer for viewing.

.txt   An ASCII text file which can be viewed with Notepad or WordPad.

Formatted Documents:

.doc   Used for formatted ASCII text files, but also for documents created in Microsoft Word or WordPerfect for Windows.

.pdf   Portable Document Format, a binary format developed by Adobe Systems, Inc. that allows formatted documents to be transferred across the Net so they look the same on any machine. Requires a Reader which is available directly from Adobe.

.ps   A PostScript file is unreadable except by a PostScript printer or with an onscreen viewer like Ghostscript.

Compressed and Encoded Files:

.arc An old binary format for archiving and compression, which can be manipulated by several programs, including the original ARC, ARCE (also known as ARC-E), PKXARC, and PKUNPAK.

.arj A binary format for MS-DOS machines, especially in Europe. You can use WinZIP, or Stuffit Expander for Windows.

.bin A Macbinary II Encoded File requiring Stuffit Expander.

.exe A DOS or Windows binary executable program or self-extracting file. Launched by double-clicking on the icon on your desktop.

.gz/gzip The GNU Project's compression program, a binary format most commonly used for UNIX and PC files. Use WinZip which handles this format the same way as Zip files.

.hqx A Macintosh binary file that has been converted into ASCII text so it can be safely transferred across the Net. Use BinHex13 (binhex13.zip) on a Windows PC to un-binhex it.

.sit A Macintosh binary file that has been compressed using the Stuffit program. Use Stuffit Expander for Windows.

.sea A Macintosh self-extracting binary archive file.

.tar/.tar.gz/.tar.Z/.tgz

These binary files are often found on Unix-based Internet sites. WinZip handles all these formats the same way as Zip files.

.uu

UUencoded binary file. Used to convert binary data into text so it can be sent via e-mail. Explorer automatically decodes this type. You can also use WinCode to UUdecode files in Windows.

.Z

A UNIX binary compression format. Use WinZIP to decompress and view files with this extension.

.zip

A common binary compression standard for DOS and Windows that uses the DOS utility PKZIP. These files can be decompressed on the PC with WinZIP.

Graphics Files:

.gif

The most common graphics file format (binary) on the Internet, it stands for Graphics Interchange Format. Explorer views these automatically, or you can use Lview Pro (lviewpxx.zip) on a Windows PC.

.jpg/jpeg/jfif

A popular binary compression standard used for photos and still images. Explorer views these automatically, or you can use Lview Pro (lviewpxx.zip) on a Windows PC.

.tiff/.tif	A very large, high-resolution binary image format. Use Lview Pro or PolyView on a Windows PC.

Sound Files:

.au/uLaw/MuLaw	The most common sound format (binary) found on the Web.
.aiff/.aif	A fairly common binary sound format found on the Web.
.ra	Real Audio, a new binary audio format, which allows you to play sounds in real-time. Requires a Real Audio Player.
.wav	The native sound format for Windows.

Video Files:

.avi	The standard binary video format for Windows.
.mov/.movie	A common binary format for QuickTime movies, the Macintosh native movie platform.
.mpg/mpeg	A standard binary format for "movies" on the Internet, using the MPEG compression scheme. There are a variety of MPEG Players for Windows and an MPEG FTP Site that has a large collection of MPEG player resources for all platforms (Mac, Windows, and UNIX).
.qt	Another extension that denotes a binary QuickTime movie file.

INDEX

NOTES

NOTES

COMPANION DISCS

There is no COMPANION DISC for this book.

COMPANION DISCS for many of the other computer books written by the same author(s) and published by BERNARD BABANI (publishing) LTD, except for the ones with an asterisk against their title in the list at the front of this book, are available.

Make sure you fill in your name and address and specify the book number and title in your order.

ORDERING INSTRUCTIONS

To obtain companion discs, fill in the order form below, or a copy of it if you don't want to spoil your book, enclose a cheque (payable to **P.R.M. Oliver**) or a postal order, and send it to the address given below.

Book No.	Book Name	Unit Price	Total Price
BP		£3.50	
BP		£3.50	
BP		£3.50	
Name		Sub-total	£.............
Address		P & P (@ 45p/disc)	£.............
		Total Due	£.............

Send to: P.R.M. Oliver, CSM, Pool, Redruth, Cornwall, TR15 3SE

PLEASE NOTE

The author(s) are fully responsible for providing this Companion Disc service. The publishers of this book accept no responsibility for the supply, quality, or magnetic contents of the disc, or in respect of any damage, or injury that might be suffered or caused by its use.